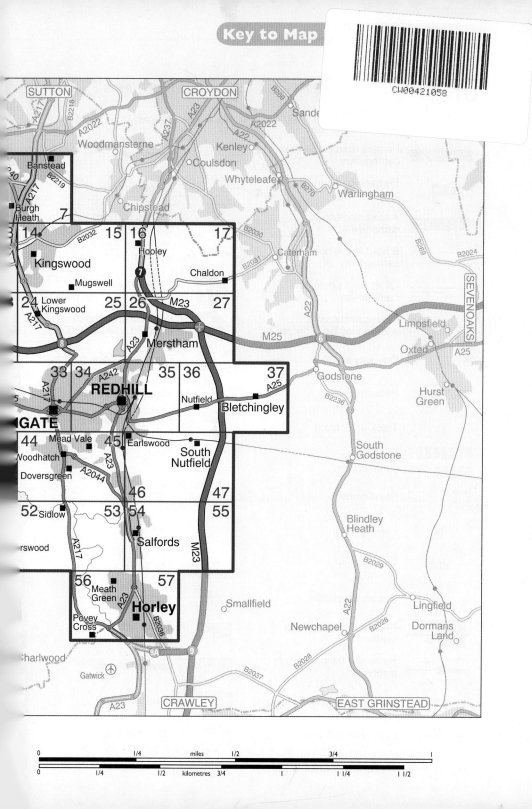

Junction 9 Motorway & junction	*LC* Level crossing
Services Motorway service area	●—●—●—● Tramway
Primary road single/dual carriageway	Ferry route
Services Primary road service area	Airport runway
A road single/dual carriageway	County, administrative boundary
B road single/dual carriageway	Mounds
Other road single/dual carriageway	**I7** Page continuation 1:15,000
Minor/private road, access may be restricted	**3** Page continuation to enlarged scale 1:10,000
← ← One-way street	River/canal, lake, pier
Pedestrian area	Aqueduct, lock, weir
Track or footpath	465 ▲ Winter Hill Peak (with height in metres)
Road under construction	Beach
Road tunnel	Woodland
P Parking	Park
P+🚌 Park & Ride	Cemetery
🚌 Bus/coach station	Built-up area
Railway & main railway station	Industrial/business building
Railway & minor railway station	Leisure building
⊖ Underground station	Retail building
⊖ Light railway & station	Other building
+++++++ Preserved private railway	

City wall	Castle
A&E	Hospital with 24-hour A&E department		Historic house or building
PO	Post Office	Wakehurst Place NT	National Trust property
	Public library	M	Museum or art gallery
i	Tourist Information Centre		Roman antiquity
i	Seasonal Tourist Information Centre		Ancient site, battlefield or monument
	Petrol station, 24 hour Major suppliers only		Industrial interest
†	Church/chapel		Garden
	Public toilets		Garden Centre Garden Centre Association Member
	Toilet with disabled facilities		Garden Centre Wyevale Garden Centre
PH	Public house AA recommended		Arboretum
	Restaurant AA inspected		Farm or animal centre
Madeira Hotel	Hotel AA inspected		Zoological or wildlife collection
	Theatre or performing arts centre		Bird collection
	Cinema		Nature reserve
	Golf course		Aquarium
▲	Camping AA inspected	V	Visitor or heritage centre
	Caravan site AA inspected		Country park
	Camping & caravan site AA inspected		Cave
	Theme park		Windmill
	Abbey, cathedral or priory		Distillery, brewery or vineyard

Epsom General Hospital

Chalk Lane Hotel

The Durdans

Council Building

Epsom Cemetery

Woodcote

Woodcote Park

Old Barn Road

The Ridge

Golf Course

Derby Stables Road

Derby Arms Rd

ASHLEY ROAD
B290

TATTENHAM CORNER
Grand Stand

Epsom Downs Racecourse

Epsom Downs

Langley Vale Road

Rosebery Road
Harding Rd
Vale Primary School
Grosvenor Road
Beaconsfield Road
Spencer Close

Miller's Copse
Langley Cl
Saddlers Way
Strand Cl
The Hayes
Yattendean
Mearnstead
St Cl

Langley Vale

Chalk Pit Road

Walton Downs

HEATH ROAD

BURGH

B290

Treadwell Road
Treadwell Rd
Milburn Wk
Worton Cl
Aston Wy
Downs Wy
Downs Way

Walnut Cl
Beech Wy

Chalk Lane

Chalk La
Chalk Paddock
Chalk La Place
Woodcote End

Axwood
Chantry Hurst
Cedar Hill
Oak Hill
Pine Hill
Warren Hill
Woodcote
Hambledon Hill
Hambledon Vale
Baron's Hurst
Sunny Bank
Hylands Rd
Diggens Rise
Epsom Park Road
Woodcote Park Road
Woodcote Green Road
Wilmerhatch Lane

B289

Nohome Farm

Ebbisham

KT18

E F G H I

E F G H

12

21 22

59 58 57

1 2 3 4 5

6

A B C D

57 512 13

Bookham Road

P

1

Great Bookham Common

Sheepbell Farm

P

Mark Oak Gate

Cobha

Langalller Lane

Ftch Cmm

2

56

Little Bookham Common

Great Mornshill Wood

The Glade

Woodside

The Glade

Revell Cl

Commonside

Bushy Rd

Westfield Drive

Barclay Close

The Copse

Meadow Way

Greenway

Willow Vale

Salix

Willow Vale

Long Copse Close

Spring Gro

Ric

3

155

Bookham Grange Hotel

Bookham Station

P

Church Road

Commonside

Leaside

Elmfield

Hambledon Place

Meadowside

Squirrels Green

Parklands Murrells

Park Way

Park Walk

Long

Vincent Cl

Eastwick

Fernlea

Maddox Pk

Bookham Industrial Estate

Bracken

Merrylands Farm

Edenslea Road

Sharon Cl

Fiona Cl

Park

The

Greenacres

Charlwood Close

Eastwick Junior School

The Spinney

4

Atwood

Maddox Road

Burnhams Road

Edgeley

Longheath Drive

Burnhams Rd

Foxl La

Lane

Lti Bookham St

Merrylands Road

Burrows

Oakdene Road

Einswood

Beattie

Twelve Acre Cl

Lime Tree Close

Mill Cl

Mill Cl

Mill Cl

Park

Church Road

Eastwick Infant School

Surgery

Eastwick Park Av

Pk

5

512

Little Bookham

Bookham St

Heatherlea Cl

Fairlawn

Sole Cl

Meadow Lane

Tudor Close

Sole Farm Road

KT23

Sole Farm Avenue

Childs

Castle Cl

Ashley Close

Sole Farm Av

Middlemead Rd

The

Mead Crs

Carstons

Middlemead Rd

Solecote

Stonehill Cl

Vicarage

The Moorings

Post Office

House

The Park

Fife Way

Church Rd

High St

Pine Walk

East St

Pine Dean

Camilla Cl

Chillmans Dr

Proctor Gar

Park vw

A B 18 C D

512 13 wer Road

Lti Bookham St

Little Rd

The Lorne

Hawkwood Rd

Wanns

Dawnay County Primary School

Infant School

Townsend

Griffin Way

Leatherhead Rd

Fairfield Medical Centre

Lthrho

HER

Great Book

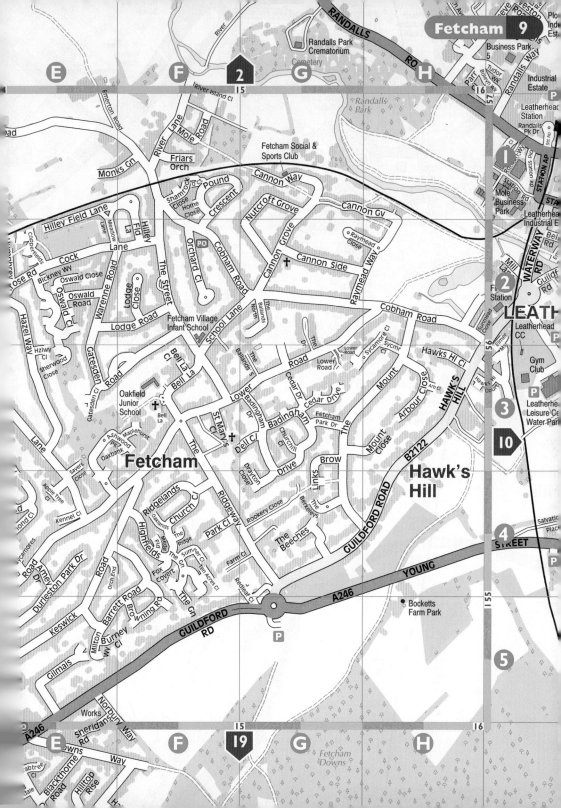

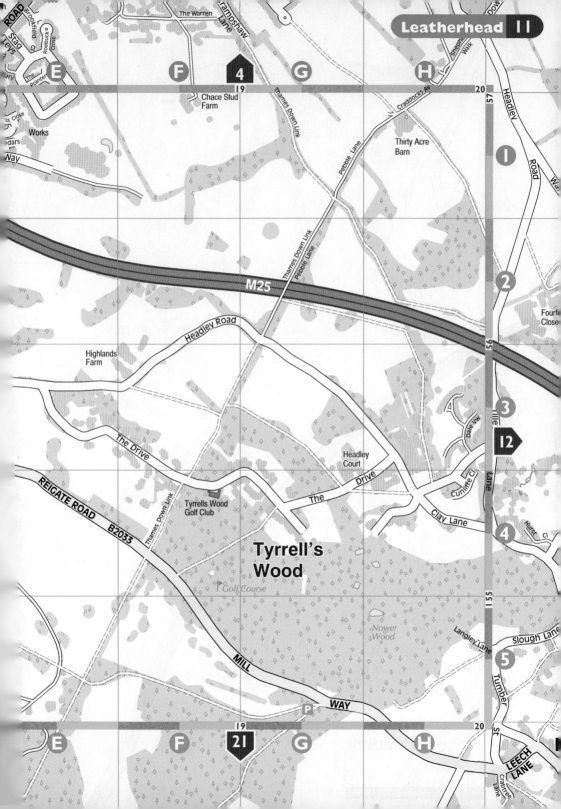

Kingswood

Golf Course

Kingswood
Golf Club

Kingswood
Warren

Kingswood Station

St Margaret's
School

Heathcote
Medical
Centre

Tudors
Business
Centre

Warren
Lodge
Drive

Holly Lodge
(Mobile Home
Park)

St Monica's Road

WATERHOUSE LANE

BONSOR DRIVE

B2032

BRIGHTON ROAD

A217

Waterhouse Lane

Forest Drive

Beechwood Av

The Glade

Warren Drive

Beeches Wd

Sandy Lane

Beeches Close

Pinehurst Cl

Chestnut Close

Beech Drive

Bears Den

Woodland

Heather Close

Glen Cl

The Warren

Hamilton Pl

Vicarage Cl

Birch Grove

Birch Gv

Eynurst Spur

Eynurst Close

Sandy Lane

Beechen Lane

Millfield Lane

Green Lane

Monkswell Lane

Chip

1st Av
2nd Av
3rd Av
4th Av
5th Av
6th Av
7th Av
8th Av
10th Av
11th Av
12th Av
13th Av
14th Av
15th Av
16th Av
Chesham Rd

Green Lane

Brier

Copley Way

Vernon Wk

Alcocks Close
Alcocks Lane

Doric Dr

The Ridings

Cedar Wk

Furze Hill

Ballantyne Dr

Hill La

Summerlay Cl

Hudsons

St Margaret's

Works

Kipings

Bayeux

Heathcote

Watt's

14

7

C

D

A

B

24

1

2

3

13

MILL

4

5

A217

B2032

PO

OUT

1 grid square represents 500 metres

OUTWOOD L

Chipstead Bottom

E

F

27 2032

G

H

High Rd Vincents ck

Castle

Chipstead
RFC

Road

Chase

Larch
Close

28 57

Golf Course

Elmore

Road

I

star

High Road

Surrey Downs
Golf Club

Eyhurst
Farm

Eyhurst
Court

Hogscross

Lane

Noke Farm

2

56

White Hill

3

16

4

Pigeonhouse
Lane

Southerns
Lane

Reeves
Rest

High Road

Markedge Lane

155

swell

Rectory Road

Park
Farm

Harps

5

Oak

Fair

Lane

Boars Gree
Farm

E

F

27

25

G

H

28

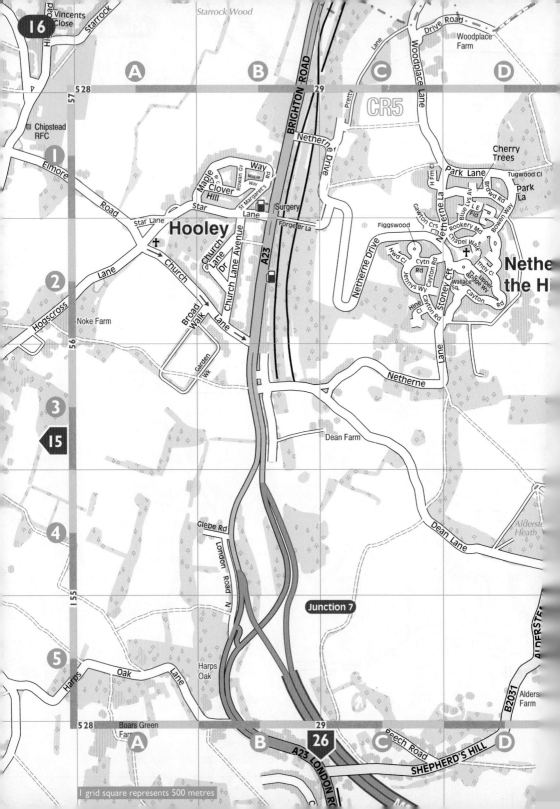

E F G H

31 **32**

Toilers Farm

Ellis Road

Lacy Crn

Goodenough Way

Weston

Middle

Goodenough

Ct

Parson's
Pightle

COULSDON
Lacey Dr

Av

Tennison
Tcl

Commonside
Cl

High
School

Stites

Purley John Fisher
FC

ROAD

B2030

57

Coulsdon C

P

Old Fox Cl

The Gro

Stirling Dr

Anglo

Stirling
Dr

Hawarden

Adair

Gdns

Weston

Haywain

Grenaway

Acdif

Rd

Gdns

Green Lane

I

London Loop

Magazine   Road

Welling

Cornwallis
Cl

2

Fa

The
Gullet

56

Croydon
Surrey County

Golf Course

3

Court Farm

†

Leazes Avenue

Surrey National
Golf Club

Fry

Church

Doctors

Lane

Lane

LANE

4

Linden
Dr

Mount
Avenue

DEAN LANE

ROOK

Chaldon

Lane

155

B2031

Hilltop
Lane

Willey Broom La

St Peter & Paul CE
Infant School

Rook Farm

Birchcroft Cl

Birchwood

5

Tollsworth
Manor

Six Brothers Field

E F **27** G H

31 **32**

Pilgrims' Lane

s Way

Westhu

Milton
Burney Cl
Gilmais

E

F

9

G

H

Works
Norbury Way
Sheridan Rd
Downs Way

D
PO
A246
Crabtree Cl
Ashdale
Blackthorne Road
Hilltop Rise
Halepit Road
Hales Oak
Crabtree Lane
Downs VW Rd

y Road
vard Road
Oakdene Close
Timber Close
South Bookham School

Fetcham Downs

I

54

2
Norbury Park

Druids Grove

3

20

53

4

Chapel Lane

Phoenice Farm

P
Crabtree Lane
Crabtree Cottage

5

152
Chapel Farm

Bagden Hill

Bagden Farm

Chapel Lane

E

F

28

G

H

15

16

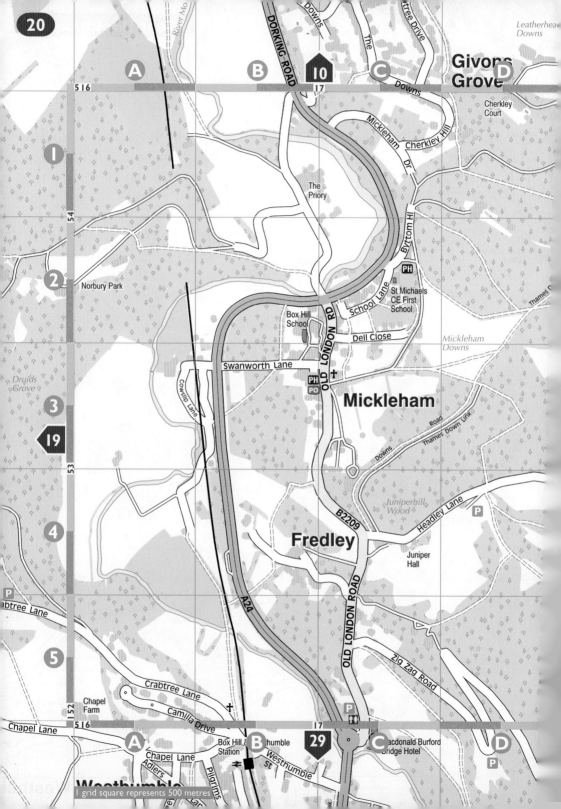

A **B** **10** **C** Givons Grove **D**

516 17

Leatherhead Downs

River Mo

DORKING ROAD

Downs

The

tree Drive

Downs

Mickleham Dr

Cherkley Hill

Cherkley Court

1

54

The Priory

Bottom Hi

2

Norbury Park

PH

St Michaels CE First School

School Lane

Box Hill School

Dell Close

Mickleham Downs

OLD LONDON RD

Swanworth Lane

PH PO

†

Mickleham

Druids Grove

3

19

53

Cowslip Lane

Road

Thames Down Link

Downs

4

B2209

Juniperhill Wood

Headley Lane

P

Fredley

Juniper Hall

5

A24

abtree Lane

P

Crabtree Lane

Chapel Farm

152

Camilla Drive

†

Zig Zag Road

Chapel Lane

516

P

17

Chapel Lane

A Chapel Lane Adlers

Box Hill & humble Station

Pilgrims

B humble Westhumble St

29

P

C acdonald Burford Bridge Hotel

D

Westhumble

P

1 grid square represents 500 metres

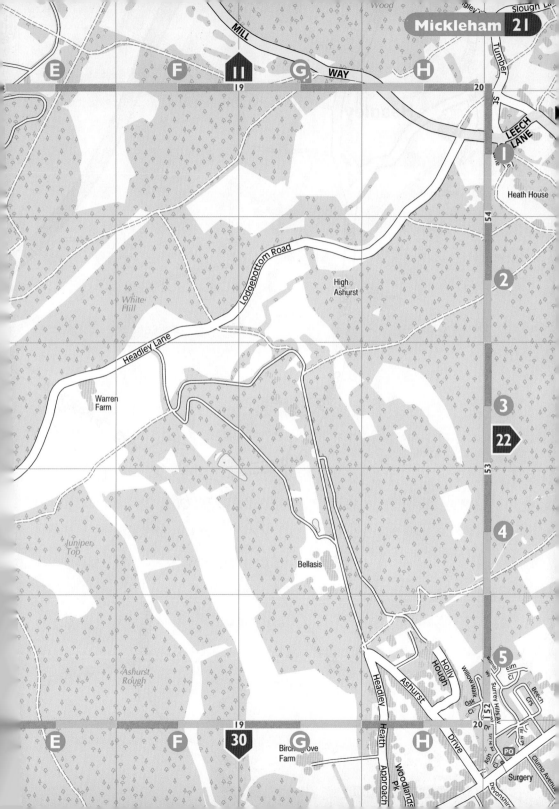

MILL WAY

E F II G WAY H

LEECH LANE

Tumber

St

19 20

Wood

Slough La

Heath House

I

54

Lodgebottom Road

High
Ashurst

2

White
Hill

Headley Lane

3

Warren
Farm

22

53

Juniper
Top

4

Bellasis

Ashurst
Rough

Holly
Hough

5

Willow Walk

Surrey Hills Av

Oak Cl

Elm Cl

Beech
Crs

E F 30 G H

19 20

Birch Grove
Farm

Headley

Ashurst

Heath

Woodlands
Pk

Approach

Drive

PO

152

Surgery

Clump Avenue

Headley

A B 12 C D

1

5 20
54

Tumber Lane

Slough

LEECH LANE
Crabtree Lane

Heath House

B2033 HEADLEY

2
54

Headley Grove

3
21
53

Heath Farm

Frith Park

M2

Love Lane

COMMON

Headley Grove

Headley Heath

ROAD

B2032 DORKING ROAD

4

Pebble Cl

Pebble Coombe

ROAD

PEBBLEHILL

North Downs Way

5
52

Holly Hough
Willow Walk
Wendal
Elm Cl
Beech Crs
Oak Cl

Boxhill Road

Maybury Farm

5 20

A B 31 C D
21

Drive

PO

Surgery

Cluma Aven

The Coombe

B2032

I grid square represents 500 metres

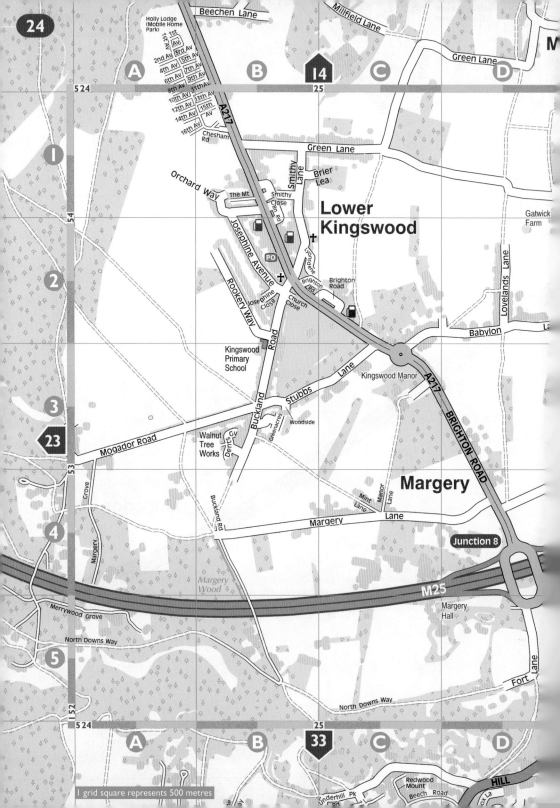

Rectory Road

gswell

Park Farm

Harps

Oak

E

Fair

F

I5

27

G

H

Boars Gr Farm

28

I

Lane

54

Upper Gatton Park

Markedge Lane

Old Mint House

2

Crossways Farm

Gatton Bottom

Whitehall Farm

Lane

Crossways

Lane

M25

3

Reigate H Golf Club

53

26

N Downs Wy

Gatton

N Downs Way

Gatton Hall

The Royal Alexandra & Albert School

4

North Downs Way

The Lake

5

-HILL

ns Way

P

Wray Lane

A217

A242

ROAD

PO

Ringwood Av

52

Holc
court

Ranmore Close

Clare
Ro

Alpi
Roac

DON ROAD

E

F

34

27

G

PARK

North Md

Colesmead

H

Monson Road

Lyndale Rd

Works

Gatton

Gatton
Close

St Bedes School

Carlton Green

**Coles
Meade**

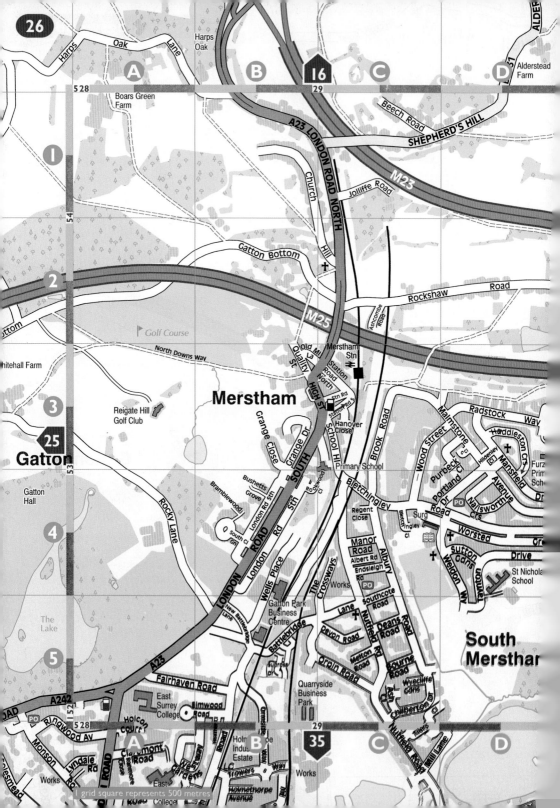

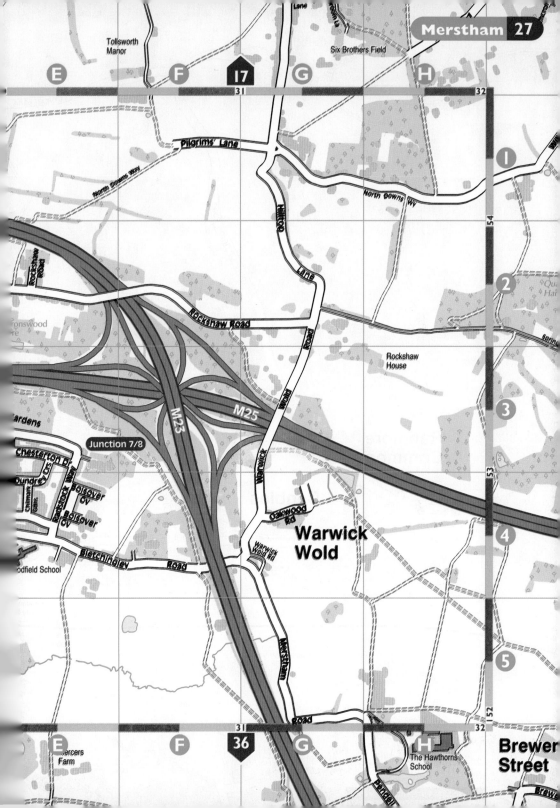

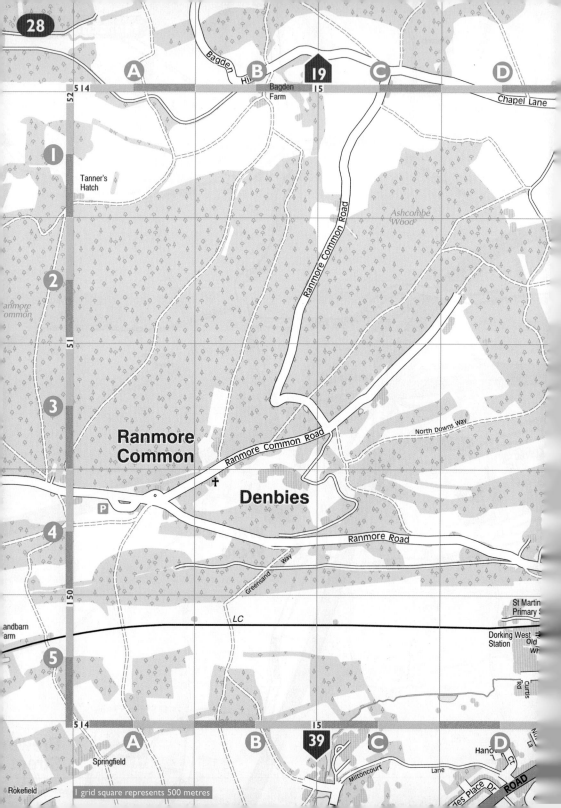

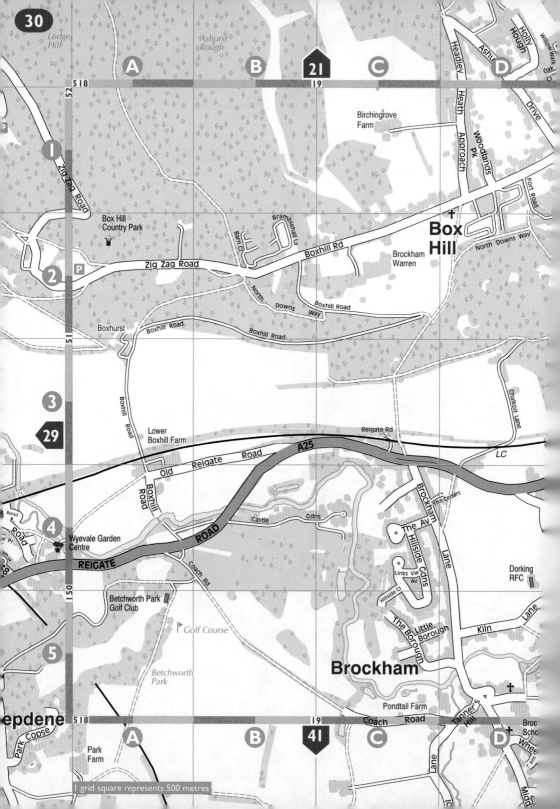

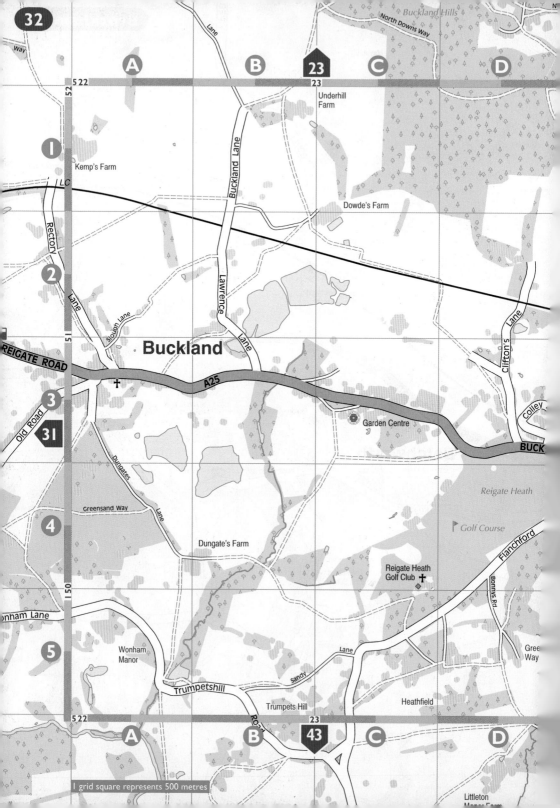

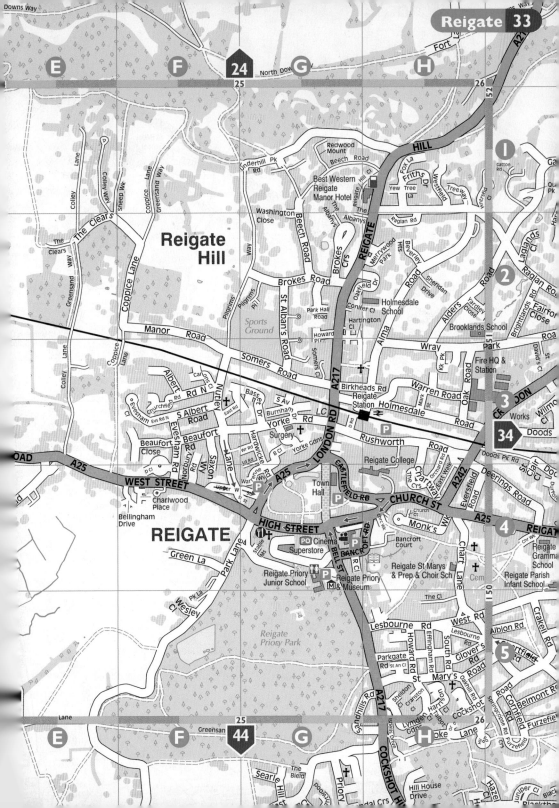

38

White
Downs

5 12

Nor... vns Way

A

B

13

C

D

Farm

Hole Hill

Rokefield

Surgery

1

49

Stockman's
Coomb
Farm

Lane

Westc...

Westcott

2

Balchins

Deerlead
Road

Th...
p...

Sandrock Road

Park
Farm

Vale
Farm

Coast Hill Lane

A25

Greensand Way

3

48

COAST HILL

Rookery Drive

The
Rookery

Westcott
Heath

West ... lane

St Johns Church Rd

Wotton

Sheephouse Lane

Sheephouse
Grn

Wolvent Lane

4

West ... Lane

5

M...
Fa...

47

Wotton Drive

Greensand Way

Hollow Lane

Wotton House

5 12

A

B

13

C

Wolvent Lane

D Lo...
Gr...

I grid square represents 500 metres

28

E F G H

RH4

Springfield

Dorking West Station
Old Char...
Station Rd

Curtis Rd
Beech Close

The Dorking
Bus Park

Curtis Road

STATION RD
WEST ST

Milton Court

Hanover
Ct

Nutcombe La

Vaughan

Howard Rd

Port Rd

Chrc st

Miltoncourt

Lane

Sondes Place Dr

WESTCOTT ROAD A25

Glebe Road

Industrial
Estate

Ebbisham
Close

St Josephs
RC Prim
School

VINCENT LA

Arundel

Vincent...

Norfol...

Surg

A29

I

Nower Road

The Priory
CE Voluntary
Aided School

Powell Corderoy
Primary School

Longfield Rd

Longfield Road

Milton
Heath

Hampstead Lane

West Bank

Vincent Drive

Ebbisham
Close

Ham

2

Miltoncourt Lane

Lince Lane

Milton Av

School

Milton Street

Westcott CE
First School

Broomfield Rd

Pointer's Hill

Stones Lane

Parsonage La

Institute Road

Hidens

RD

ORD

ROAD

PO

St John's Rd

The Burtell

Chapel La

Furlong Road

Watson Road

Ashley Road

Bailey Road

ngfield Road

...hurst
Close

Greensand Way

The Nower

Home
Farm

3

Harr...
Close

Knol

Ridgeway Cl

Ridge Wa

40

48

4

49

5

Westlees
Farm

Chadhurst
Farm

E F G H

47

15 16

15 16

15 16

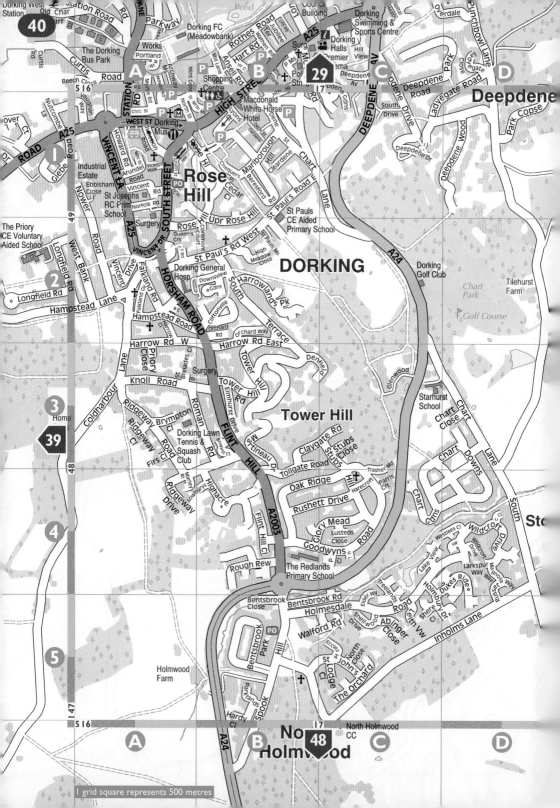

Brockham

E F 30 G H

I Golf Course

Betchworth Park

Pondtail Farm

Coach Road

Tanner's Hill

Brockham School

Wheelers La

Dodds Pk

Park Farm

School Lane

Brockham School

Warrenne Road

Oakdene Rd

Wheelers Lane

Oakdene Cl

Tilehurst Lane

Lands

Old School Lane

Felton's Farm

Moat House Farm **2**

Tanner's Brook

Glenfield Road

Glenfield Close

Brent House Rd

Silverdale Close

Tanners Meadow

Surgery

3

Boxhill Way

Tynedale Rd

The Cl

Jubilee Terrace **42**

Parkpale Lane

Bushbury

Ridge Cl

Tweed Lane

Tweed Lane

Park Cl

Middle Street

dge

Bushbury Lane

4

Coleshill Farm

Bushbury

Roothill

5

Roothill

Middle Street

Leiyn R

E F 49 G H Road 20

Blackbrook

Great Brockhamhurst

Brockhamh

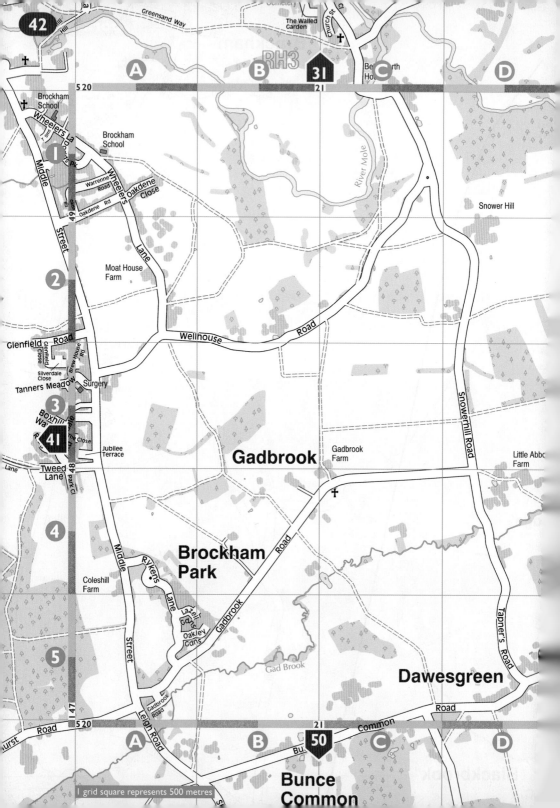

Wonham Manor

Lane

Sandy

Trumpetshill

E

Trumpets I

F

32
23

G

Heathfield

H

Littleton Lane

I

Littleton Manor Farm

49

Wallace Brook

2

Clayhall Lane

Ricebridge Farm

Flanchford Road

Santon House

Flanchford Farm

3

44

48

Little Flanchford

Flanchford Road

4

River Mole

Leigh Place

Leigh Place Road

Burys Court School

5

I 47

ool

E

PH

Glen

Harrington Close

†

F

51
23

G

H

24

Bures Manor

gh

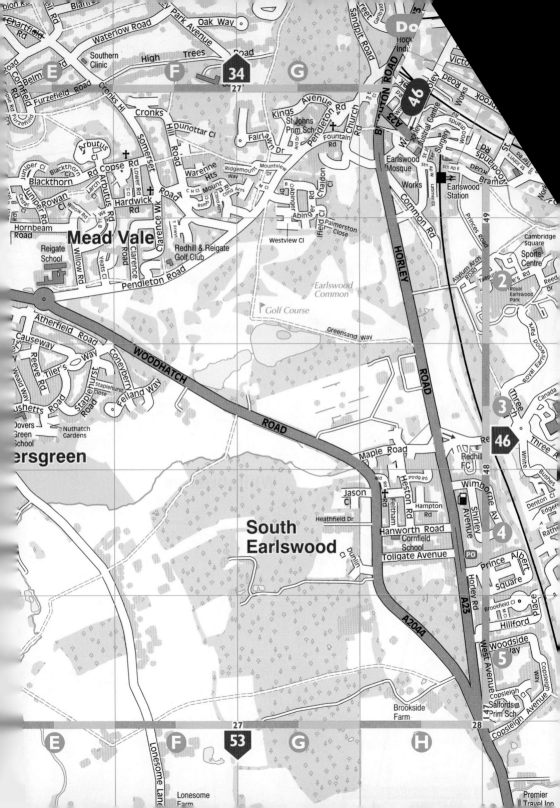

Woodside

Sylvan Way
Hillview dr
Redstone Lane
Rennie Ter
Mostyn Ter
Linnell Road
Philanthropic dr

Philanthropic   Road

Hogtrough Lane

Sand

A   **B**   Redstone   **C**   Clay Lane   **D**
Cemetery
Re...e College
35
29

Bower Hill Lane

5 28
John... st
Emlyn Road
Ifold Road
Althorne Road
Knighton Road
Trentham Rd

Hartspiece Rd
Ash Drive
Willow Walk
Willow Dve
C C Road
Chs
Chs Crs
Oakland...
Crofters Close

Haigh Cl

Haw...n Rd

Eastfield Road

Earlswood

PO
Stn Ap E

I

Earlswood
Station

Brambletye Park Road

Brambletye
Junior
School

Common Rd
Princes Road
49

Cambridge Square
Palmerston Close

Sports Centre

Talfourd Wy
Prince's Rd
m Arch 3rd

Reed Dve

2

Royal Earlswood Park

Gatehouse Lodge

Golf Driving Range

Royal Park Road
Royal Earls...

Three Arch Rd

Canada Avenue

A&E
East Surrey
Hospital

3

ROAD
A2044

45
Redhill
FC
48

Reigate Rd

Three Arch Rd

White
Bushes

Wimborne Av

Hampton Rd
ptrdg Rd

Shirley Ave

4

PO

Denton Cl
Edgefield Cl
Rathgar Cl

Bushfield Drive

Hawthorn Rd
Cranford Cl
Crantwo Dr
Ambled Cl
Yeoman Way
Lunar Cl
...wydene

Mason's

Kings Mill Lane

Whitebushes

Spencer
Jordans Cl
Greenwood dr
Green Lane

Wydene

Way

Bridge

North Road
Thornfield School

Prince Albert
Square

Brookfield Cl

Hillford

Horley Rd
A23

Place

5

West Avenue
Woodside Way

Copsleigh Avenue
Way

Copsleigh
Salfords
Prim Sch

147
5 28
Copsleigh Avenue

okside

A2044

A   **B** ean Farm   **C**   **D**
29
54

1 grid square represents 500 metres

Travel Inn

Greensand Way

Kentwyns Rise

Braes Md

Nutfield Church CE Primary School

36

Lyttel Hall

Cooper's Hill Rd

Greensand Way

Sandhills Farm

E

F

31

G

H

32

South Nutfield

Greensand Way

Nutfield Station

Holmesdale Road

Trindles Road

Mid Street

PO

I

49

Kings Mead

The Copse

Morris Rd

St Ap

Cricket Hl

South Nutfield CC

Bower Hill Close

Netherleigh Park

The Avenue

RH1

2

Ridge Green

Thepps Cl

Ridge Grn

Kings Cross Lane

Nutfield Pk

Cooper's Hl Rd

Henshaw Farm

Ridge Green

Crab Hill Farm

Cooper's Hill Road

3

48

edhill erodrome

Crab Hill Lane

4

Burstow Park Farm

5

Moats Lane

Lane

South Hale Farm

Hatch La

I 47

Moats

Lane

Moats

E

F

31

55

G

Wales Road

H

32

M23

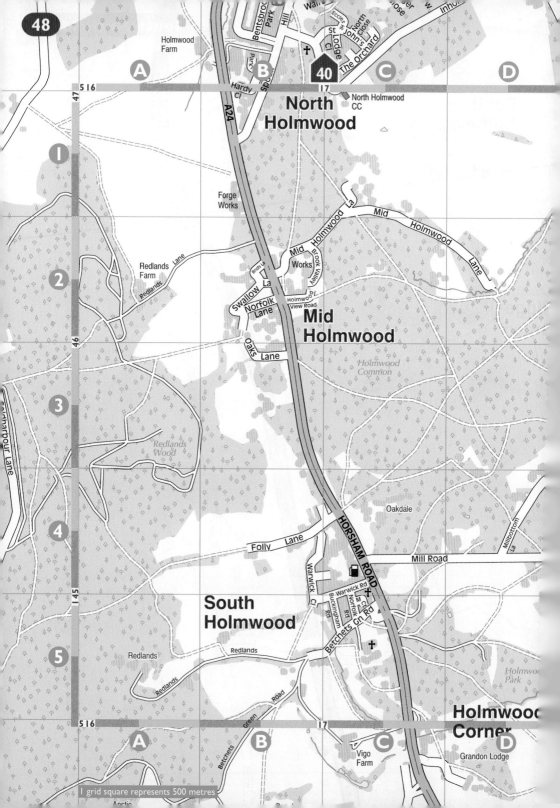

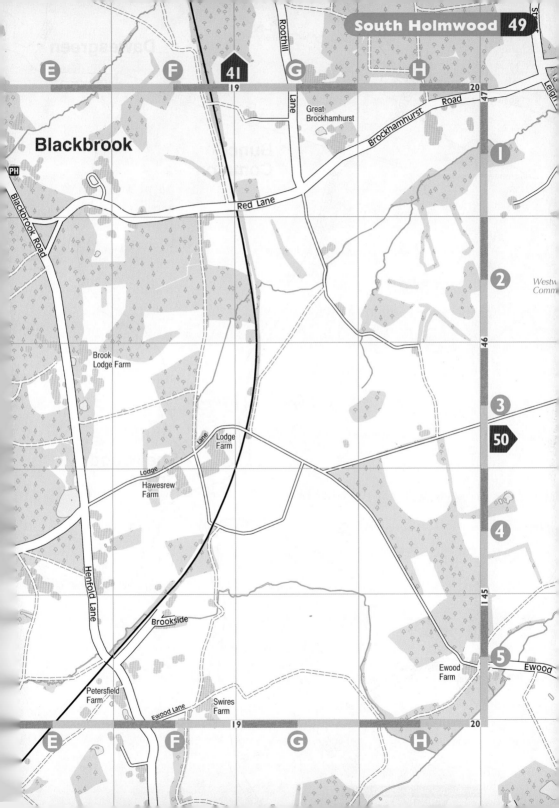

E F **41** G H

19

20

Blackbrook

PH

Blackbrook Road

Roothill Lane

Lane

Great Brockhamhurst

Brockhamhurst Road

Leigh

47

I

Red Lane

2

Westw Comm

46

Brook Lodge Farm

3

50

Lane

Lodge Farm

Lodge

Hawesrew Farm

4

145

Henfold Lane

Brookside

5

Ewood Farm

Ewood

Petersfield Farm

Ewood Lane

Swires Farm

E F G H

19

20

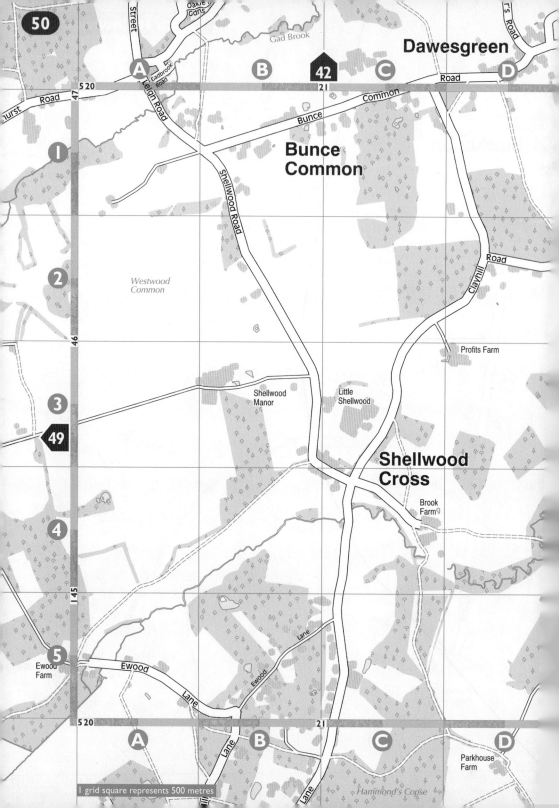

E   F   **43**   G   H

23   24   47

Burys Court
School

rns
School

PH

The Glebe

Harrington
Close

eigh

Clayhill
Cl

Clayhill Farm

Leigh Place Road

Bures
Manor

I

Swains Farm

Dene
Farm

2

Stumblehole
Farm

46

3

52

Deanoak Lane

Nalderswood

Mynthurst

Grove
Farm

4

Smalls Hill Road

145

5 Dean
Business
Park

23   24

E   F   G   Norwood
Place Farm   H

oak B

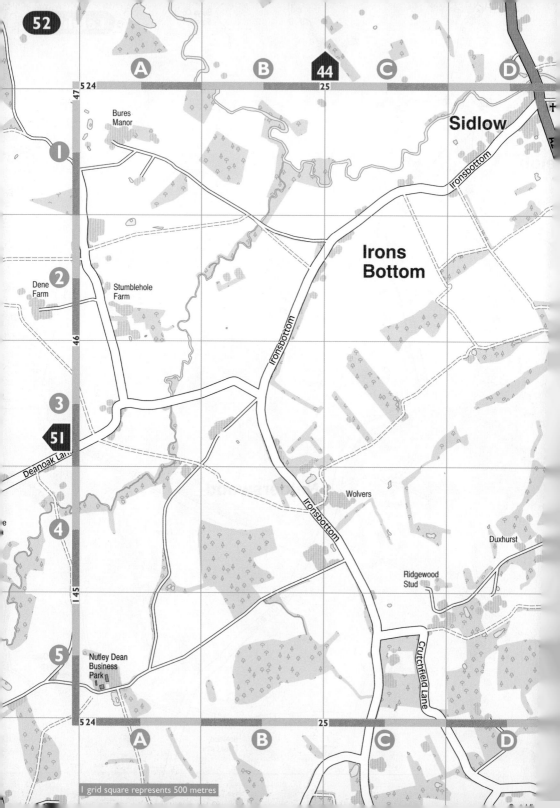

A   B   44   C   D

5 24   47   25

Sidlow

Bures
Manor

1

Ironsbottom

2

Dene
Farm

Stumblehole
Farm

**Irons
Bottom**

Ironsbottom

46

3

51

Deanoak Lane

Wolvers

4

Duxhurst

145

Ridgewood
Stud

Ironsbottom

5

Nutley Dean
Business
Park

Crutchfield Lane

5 24   25

A   B   C   D

I grid square represents 500 metres

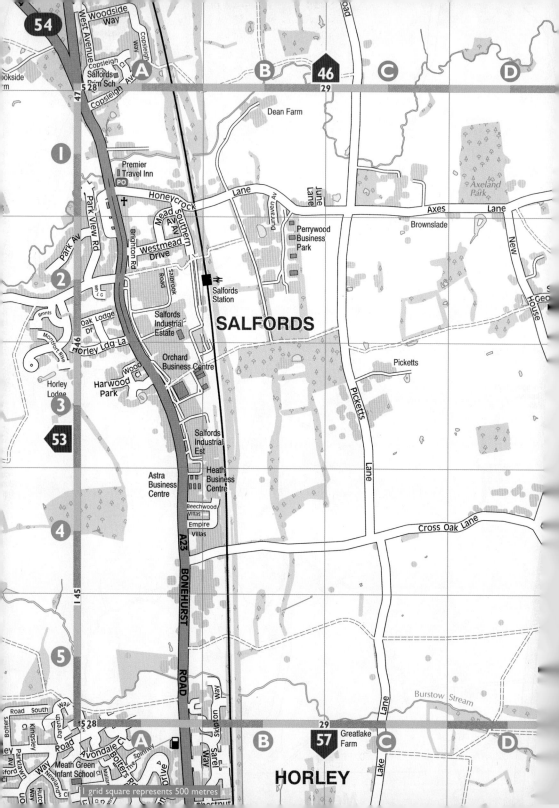

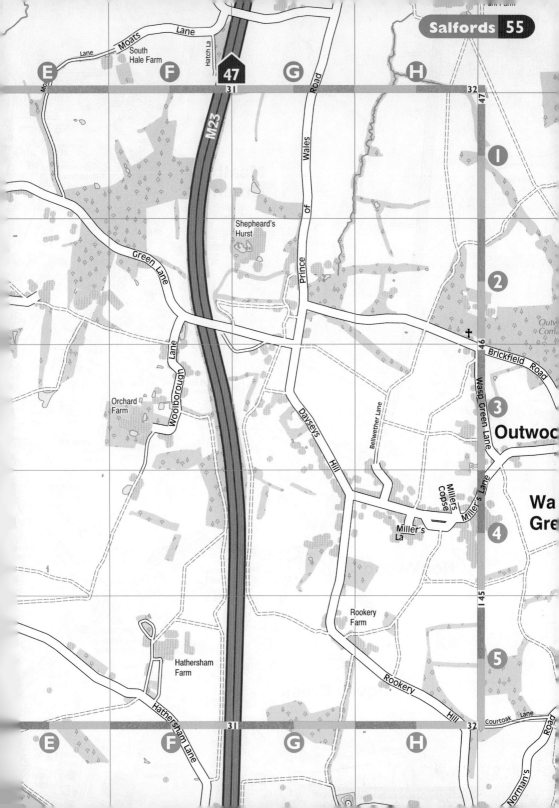

E **F** 47 **G** **H**

Moats Lane

Lane

South Hale Farm

Hatch La

M23

Wales Road

Prince of

I

Shepheard's Hurst

Green Lane

2

Outv
Com

Brickfield Road

Woolborough Lane

Orchard Farm

Dalseys Hill

Bellwether Lane

Wasp Green Lane

3

Outwo

Miller's Copse

Miller's Lane

**Wa
Gre**

Miller's La

4

Rookery Farm

5

Hathersham Farm

Rookery Hill

Courtoak Lane

Norman's Road

E **F** **G** **H**

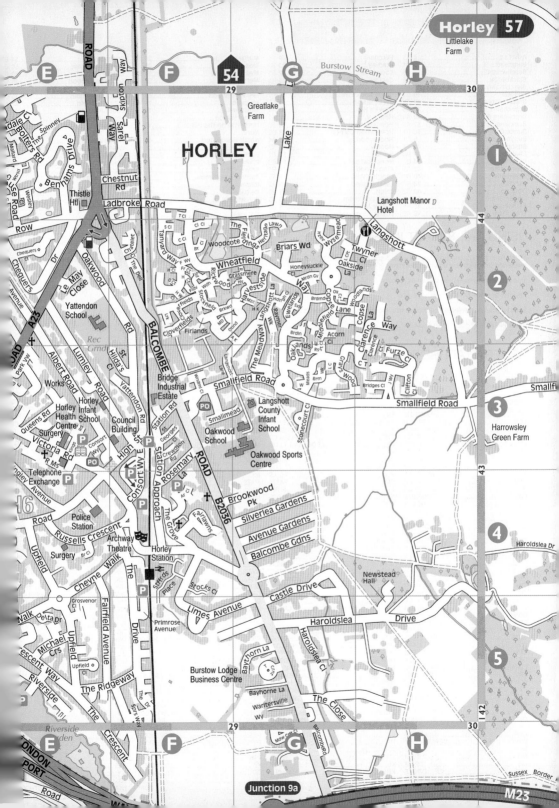

Ashtead	4	A3	Fetcham	9	F3	Margery	24	C4	Salfords	54	B
Banstead	7	G1	Fredley	20	B4	Mead Vale	45	E2	Shellwood Cross	50	C
Betchworth	31	E3	Gadbrook	42	B3	Meath Green	56	B1	Sidlow	52	D
Blackbrook	49	E1	Gatton	25	H3	Merstham	26	B3	South Earlswood	45	G
Bletchingley	37	F4	Givons Grove	10	D5	Mickleham	20	C3	South Holmwood	48	B
Box Hill	30	C2	Great Bookham	18	D1	Mid Holmwood	48	B2	South Merstham	26	D
Brewer Street	37	E1	Great Burgh	6	C2	Mogador	23	H4	South Nutfield	47	E
Brockham	30	C5	Hawk's Hill	9	H4	Mugswell	14	D5	South Park	44	A
Brockham Park	42	A4	Headley	22	A1	Nalderswood	51	G4	Stonebridge	40	D
Buckland	32	A3	Holmethorpe	35	F2	Netherne on the Hill	16	D2	Tadworth	13	G
Bunce Common	50	B1	Holmwood Corner	48	D5	Nork	6	D1	Tower Hill	40	E
Burgh Heath	6	D4	Hookwood	56	A4	North Holmwood	48	B1	Tyrrell's Wood	11	C
Bushbury	41	G4	Hooley	16	A2	Nutfield	36	B4	Walton on the Hill	12	D
Chaldon	17	H4	Horley	57	F1	Pachesham Park	3	E1	Warwick Wold	27	C
Coles Meads	34	D1	Irons Bottom	52	C2	Pixham	29	G3	Westcott	38	D
Dawesgreen	42	C5	Kingswood	14	B3	Povey Cross	56	A5	Westhumble	29	E
Deepdene	40	D1	Langley Vale	5	F5	Ranmore Common	28	A3	Whitebushes	46	C
Denbies	28	B4	Leatherhead	10	A2	Redhill	35	E2	Woodcote	5	F
Dorking	40	B2	Leigh	51	E1	Reigate	33	F4	Woodhatch	44	C
Doversgreen	44	D3	Little Bookham	8	A5	Reigate Hill	33	F2	Wotton	38	A
Earlswood	45	H1	Lower Ashtead	3	G4	Ridge Green	47	E2	Wray Common	34	D
Effingham	18	A2	Lower Kingswood	24	C1	Rose Hill	40	A1			

USING THE STREET INDEX

Street names are listed alphabetically. Each street name is followed by its postal town or area locality, the Postcode District, the page number, and the reference to the square in which the name is found.

Standard index entries are shown as follows:

Abbotts Ri *REDH* RH1 ....**35** E2

Street names and selected addresses not shown on the map due to scale restrictions are shown in the index with an asterisk:

Angel Pl *REIG* RH2 * **44** D1

GENERAL ABBREVIATIONS

ACC	ACCESS	E	EAST	LDG	LODGE	R	RIV
ALY	ALLEY	EMB	EMBANKMENT	LGT	LIGHT	RBT	ROUNDABC
AP	APPROACH	EMBY	EMBASSY	LK	LOCK	RD	RC
AR	ARCADE	ESP	ESPLANADE	LKS	LAKES	RDG	RID
ASS	ASSOCIATION	EST	ESTATE	LNDG	LANDING	REP	REPUE
AV	AVENUE	EX	EXCHANGE	LTL	LITTLE	RES	RESERV
BCH	BEACH	EXPY	EXPRESSWAY	LWR	LOWER	RFC	RUGBY FOOTBALL CL
BLDS	BUILDINGS	EXT	EXTENSION	MAG	MAGISTRATE	RI	RI
BND	BEND	F/O	FLYOVER	MAN	MANSIONS	RP	RA
BNK	BANK	FC	FOOTBALL CLUB	MD	MEAD	RW	RW
BR	BRIDGE	FK	FORK	MDW	MEADOWS	S	SO
BRK	BROOK	FLD	FIELD	MEM	MEMORIAL	SCH	SCH
BTM	BOTTOM	FLDS	FIELDS	MI	MILL	SE	SOUTH E
BUS	BUSINESS	FLS	FALLS	MKT	MARKET	SER	SERVICE AI
BVD	BOULEVARD	FM	FARM	MKTS	MARKETS	SH	SH
BY	BYPASS	FT	FORT	ML	MALL	SHOP	SHOPP
CATH	CATHEDRAL	FTS	FLATS	MNR	MANOR	SKWY	SKY
CEM	CEMETERY	FWY	FREEWAY	MS	MEWS	SMT	SUM
CEN	CENTRE	FY	FERRY	MSN	MISSION	SOC	SOC
CFT	CROFT	GA	GATE	MT	MOUNT	SP	S
CH	CHURCH	GAL	GALLERY	MTN	MOUNTAIN	SPR	SPF
CHA	CHASE	GDN	GARDEN	MTS	MOUNTAINS	SQ	SQU
CHYD	CHURCHYARD	GDNS	GARDENS	MUS	MUSEUM	ST	STF
CIR	CIRCLE	GLD	GLADE	MWY	MOTORWAY	STN	STAT
CIRC	CIRCUS	GLN	GLEN	N	NORTH	STR	STR
CL	CLOSE	GN	GREEN	NE	NORTH EAST	STRD	STR
CLFS	CLIFFS	GND	GROUND	NW	NORTH WEST	SW	SOUTH V
CMP	CAMP	GRA	GRANGE	O/P	OVERPASS	TDG	TRA
CNR	CORNER	GRG	GARAGE	OFF	OFFICE	TER	TERF
CO	COUNTY	GT	GREAT	ORCH	ORCHARD	THWY	THROUGH
COLL	COLLEGE	GTWY	GATEWAY	OV	OVAL	TNL	TUI
COM	COMMON	GV	GROVE	PAL	PALACE	TOLL	TOL
COMM	COMMISSION	HGR	HIGHER	PAS	PASSAGE	TPK	TURN
CON	CONVENT	HL	HILL	PAV	PAVILION	TR	TI
COT	COTTAGE	HLS	HILLS	PDE	PARADE	TRL	T
COTS	COTTAGES	HO	HOUSE	PH	PUBLIC HOUSE	TWR	TC
CP	CAPE	HOL	HOLLOW	PK	PARK	U/P	UNDER
CPS	COPSE	HOSP	HOSPITAL	PKWY	PARKWAY	UNI	UNIVEF
CR	CREEK	HRB	HARBOUR	PL	PLACE	UPR	U
CREM	CREMATORIUM	HTH	HEATH	PLN	PLAIN	V	V
CRS	CRESCENT	HTS	HEIGHTS	PLNS	PLAINS	VA	VA
CSWY	CAUSEWAY	HVN	HAVEN	PLZ	PLAZA	VIAD	VIA
CT	COURT	HWY	HIGHWAY	POL	POLICE STATION	VIL	V
CTRL	CENTRAL	IMP	IMPERIAL	PR	PRINCE	VIS	VI
CTS	COURTS	IN	INLET	PREC	PRECINCT	VLG	VIL
CTYD	COURTYARD	IND EST	INDUSTRIAL ESTATE	PREP	PREPARATORY	VLS	V
CUTT	CUTTINGS	INF	INFIRMARY	PRIM	PRIMARY	VW	V
CV	COVE	INFO	INFORMATION	PROM	PROMENADE	W	V
CYN	CANYON	INT	INTERCHANGE	PRS	PRINCESS	WD	V
DEPT	DEPARTMENT	IS	ISLAND	PRT	PORT	WHF	W
DL	DALE	JCT	JUNCTION	PT	POINT	WK	W
DM	DAM	JTY	JETTY	PTH	PATH	WKS	W
DR	DRIVE	KG	KING	PZ	PIAZZA	WLS	W
DRO	DROVE	KNL	KNOLL	QD	QUADRANT	WY	W
DRY	DRIVEWAY	L	LAKE	QU	QUEEN	YD	Y
DWGS	DWELLINGS	LA	LANE	QY	QUAY	YHA	YOUTH H

POSTCODE TOWNS AND AREA ABBREVIATIONS

ASHTD................Ashtead	CTHM.....................Caterham	GT/LBKH...........Great Bookham/	LHD/OX............Leatherhead/Oxshott
BNSTD...............Banstead	DORK.....................Dorking	Little Bookham	RDKG........................Rural Dorking
BRKHM/BTCW...Brockham/Betchworth	EHSLY................East Horsley	HORL............................Horley	REDH.............................Redhill
COB........................Cobham	EPSOM..................Epsom	KWD/TDW/WH................Kingswood/	REIG..............................Reigate
COUL/CHIP.........Coulsdon/Chipstead	EW.........................Ewell	Tadworth/Walton on the Hill	

Index - streets

1st - Bro

1

st Av KWD/TDW/WH KT20	14 A5
d Av KWD/TDW/WH KT20	14 A5
d Av KWD/TDW/WH KT20	14 A5
h Av KWD/TDW/WH KT20	14 A5
h Av KWD/TDW/WH KT20	14 A5
h Av KWD/TDW/WH KT20	14 A5
h Av KWD/TDW/WH KT20	14 A5
h Av KWD/TDW/WH KT20	24 A1
h Av KWD/TDW/WH KT20	24 A1
th Av KWD/TDW/WH KT20	24 A1
th Av KWD/TDW/WH KT20	14 A5
th Av KWD/TDW/WH KT20	24 A1
th Av KWD/TDW/WH KT20	24 A1
th Av KWD/TDW/WH KT20	24 A1
th Av KWD/TDW/WH KT20	24 A1

A

botts Ri REDH RH1 ... 35 E2
nger Cl RDKG RH5 ... 40 C5
nger Dr REDH RH1 ... 45 G1
nger Rd REDH RH1 ... 45 G2
rn Cl HORL RH6 ... 57 G2
rn Gv KWD/TDW/WH KT20 ... 14 B4
es Gdns
  WD/TDW/WH KT20 ... 6 C4
ers La RDKG RH5 ... 29 E1
tes La LHD/OX KT22 ... 3 H1
any Park Rd LHD/OX KT22 ... 3 E4
Albanys REIG RH2 ... 33 G2
ertine Cl EW KT17 ... 6 B1
ert Rd ASHTD KT21 ... 4 B3
  ORL RH6 ... 57 E3
  EDH RH1 ... 26 C4
ert Rd North REIG RH2 ... 33 F3
on Ms REIG RH2 * ... 45 E1
on Rd REIG RH2 ... 34 A5
ry Keep HORL RH6 ... 57 F2
ry Rd REDH RH1 ... 26 C4
cks Cl KWD/TDW/WH KT20 ... 7 E5
cks La KWD/TDW/WH KT20 ... 7 F5
rs Rd REIG RH2 ... 33 H2
rstead La REDH RH1 ... 16 D5
ander Godley Cl
  SHTD KT21 ... 4 B4
ander Rd REIG RH2 ... 44 C2
a Rd GT/LBKH KT23 ... 18 D1
gham Rd REIG RH2 ... 44 C2
n Gv KWD/TDW/WH KT20 ... 13 F1
g Rd REIG RH2 ... 33 H3
e Rd REDH RH1 ... 35 E1
orne Rd REDH RH1 ... 46 A1
eside Cl REDH RH1 ... 46 B4
y Dr GT/LBKH KT23 ... 9 H5
l Pl REIG RH2 * ... 44 D1
l Rd DORK RH4 ... 29 F5
dele La LHD/OX KT22 ... 3 E3
r Rd REIG RH2 ... 44 C2
rlie Dr BRKHM/BTCW RH3 ... 31 E5
e Tree Cl LHD/OX KT22 ... 9 E4
Cl ASHTD KT21 ... 4 B3
a Cl LHD/OX KT22 ... 11 E1
r Cl LHD/OX KT22 ... 9 H3
cus Cl REDH RH1 ... 45 E1
cus Rd REDH RH1 ... 45 E1
rcade REDH RH1 * ... 35 E3
vay Ms DORK RH4 ... 29 E5
Cl REIG RH2 ... 44 D3
iel Dr REDH RH1 ... 45 G1
Gv HORL RH6 ... 56 C1
iel Rd DORK RH4 ... 40 A1
  KWD/TDW/WH KT20 ... 31 E1
  REDH RH1 ... 26 C5
mbe Rd DORK RH4 ... 29 E4
H RH1 ... 26 C2

Ashcombe Ter
  KWD/TDW/WH KT20 ... 6 B5
Ashdale GT/LBKH KT23 ... 19 E1
Ashdown Cl REIG RH2 ... 44 D3
Ashdown Rd REIG RH2 ... 44 D3
Ash Dr REDH RH1 ... 46 A1
Ashleigh Cl HORL RH6 ... 56 D3
Ashley Cl GT/LBKH KT23 ... 8 B5
Ashley Cottages ASHTD KT21 * ... 4 B4
Ashley Rd DORK RH4 ... 39 E2
  EPSOM KT18 ... 5 H1
Ashtead Woods Rd ASHTD KT21 ... 3 H1
Ashurst Cl LHD/OX KT22 ... 10 A1
Ashurst Dr KWD/TDW/WH KT20 ... 21 H5
Ashurst Pl DORK RH4 ... 29 C5
Ashurst Rd KWD/TDW/WH KT20 ... 13 F1
Ashwood Pk LHD/OX KT22 ... 9 E3
Astede Pl ASHTD KT21 ... 4 B3
Aston Cl ASHTD KT21 ... 3 G3
Aston Wy EPSOM KT18 ... 5 H1
Asylum Arch Rd REDH RH1 ... 45 H2
Atherfield Rd REIG RH2 ... 45 E2
Atkinson Ct HORL RH6 * ... 57 F4
Atwood GT/LBKH KT23 ... 8 A4
Aurum Cl HORL RH6 ... 57 F4
Avenue Cl KWD/TDW/WH KT20 ... 13 F2
Avenue Gdns HORL RH6 ... 57 G4
The Avenue BRKHM/BTCW RH3 ... 30 C4
  HORL RH6 ... 56 D4
  KWD/TDW/WH KT20 ... 13 F2
  REDH RH1 ... 47 E2
Avondale Cl HORL RH6 ... 56 D1
Axes La REDH RH1 ... 54 C1

B

Babylon La KWD/TDW/WH KT20 ... 24 D2
Baden Dr HORL RH6 ... 56 C2
Badingham Dr LHD/OX KT22 ... 9 G4
Bagden Hl RDKG RH5 ... 19 F5
Bagot Cl ASHTD KT21 ... 4 B1
Bailey Rd DORK RH4 ... 39 E2
Bakehouse Rd HORL RH6 ... 56 D1
Balchins La DORK RH4 ... 38 C2
Balcombe Gdns HORL RH6 ... 57 G4
Balcombe Rd HORL RH6 ... 57 F2
The Ballands North
  LHD/OX KT22 ... 9 G2
The Ballands' South
  LHD/OX KT22 ... 9 G3
Ballantyne Dr
  KWD/TDW/WH KT20 ... 14 B1
Ballards Gn KWD/TDW/WH KT20 ... 7 E4
Balquhain Cl ASHTD KT21 ... 3 H2
Bancroft Ct REIG RH2 ... 33 H4
Bancroft Rd REIG RH2 ... 33 G4
Barclay Cl LHD/OX KT22 ... 8 D3
Barfields REDH RH1 ... 36 D3
Barley Mow Ct
  BRKHM/BTCW RH3 ... 31 E4
Barn Cl KWD/TDW/WH KT20 ... 30 B2
Barnett Cl LHD/OX KT22 ... 3 F4
Barnett Wood La ASHTD KT22 ... 3 F4
Barn Meadow La GT/LBKH KT23 ... 8 B5
The Barnyard
  KWD/TDW/WH KT20 ... 13 E4
Baron's Hurst EPSOM KT18 ... 5 E1
Baron's Wy REIG RH2 ... 44 A4
Barrett Rd LHD/OX KT22 ... 9 E5
Barrington Ct DORK RH4 ... 40 A2
Barrington Rd DORK RH4 ... 40 A2
Bartholemew Ct DORK RH4 * ... 40 A2
Basset Dr REIG RH2 ... 33 G3
Battlebridge La REDH RH1 ... 26 B5
Batts Hl REIG RH2 ... 34 C3
Baxter Av REDH RH1 ... 34 C4
Bay Cl HORL RH6 ... 53 G5
Bayeux KWD/TDW/WH KT20 ... 13 H2
Bayfield Rd HORL RH6 ... 56 C2
Bayhorne La HORL RH6 ... 57 G5

Baythorn La HORL RH6 ... 57 G5
Bay Tree Av LHD/OX KT22 ... 3 E5
Beacon Cl BNSTD SM7 ... 6 D1
Beaconsfield Rd EPSOM KT18 ... 5 F4
Beacon Wy BNSTD SM7 ... 6 D1
Beales Rd GT/LBKH KT23 ... 18 D2
Bears Den KWD/TDW/WH KT20 ... 14 B2
Beattie Cl GT/LBKH KT23 ... 8 B4
Beauclare Cl LHD/OX KT22 ... 10 D1
Beaufort Cl REIG RH2 ... 33 F3
Beaufort Rd REIG RH2 ... 33 F3
Beaumonts REDH RH1 ... 53 H2
Beech Cl DORK RH4 ... 28 D5
Beech Crs KWD/TDW/WH KT20 ... 22 A5
Beechcroft ASHTD KT21 ... 4 B4
Beechdene
  KWD/TDW/WH KT20 ... 13 F2
Beech Dr KWD/TDW/WH KT20 ... 14 B2
  REIG RH2 ... 34 B4
Beechen La
  KWD/TDW/WH KT20 ... 14 B5
Beeches Cl KWD/TDW/WH KT20 ... 14 C3
The Beeches BNSTD SM7 ... 7 H1
  LHD/OX KT22 ... 9 G4
Beeches Wd
  KWD/TDW/WH KT20 ... 14 C2
Beech Gv EPSOM KT18 ... 6 B2
  GT/LBKH KT23 ... 18 C2
Beech Holt LHD/OX KT22 ... 10 C2
Beech Rd REDH RH1 ... 26 C1
  REIG RH2 ... 33 G2
Beechwood
  KWD/TDW/WH KT20 * ... 30 D1
Beechwood Av
  KWD/TDW/WH KT20 ... 14 C1
Beechwood Pk LHD/OX KT22 ... 10 C2
Beechwood Vls REDH RH1 ... 54 A4
Beehive Wy REIG RH2 ... 44 D3
The Belfry REDH RH1 ... 34 D3
Bell Crs COUL/CHIP CR5 ... 16 B1
Bellingham Dr REIG RH2 ... 33 F4
Bell La LHD/OX KT22 ... 9 F3
Bell Lane Cl LHD/OX KT22 ... 9 F3
Bell St REIG RH2 ... 33 G4
Bellwether La REDH RH1 ... 55 H3
Belmont Rd LHD/OX KT22 ... 10 A2
  REIG RH2 ... 34 A5
Benhams Dr HORL RH6 ... 57 E1
Bennetts Farm Pl GT/LBKH KT23 ... 8 B5
Bentsbrook Cl RDKG RH5 ... 40 B5
Bentsbrook Pk RDKG RH5 ... 40 B5
Bentsbrook Rd RDKG RH5 ... 40 B5
Beresford Rd DORK RH4 ... 40 B1
Berkeley Pl EPSOM KT18 ... 5 F1
The Berkeleys LHD/OX KT22 ... 9 G4
Berry Meade ASHTD KT21 ... 4 B2
Berry Meade Cl ASHTD KT21 ... 4 B2
Berry Wk ASHTD KT21 ... 4 B4
Betchets Green Rd RDKG RH5 ... 48 C5
Beverley Hts REIG RH2 ... 33 H2
Bickney Wy LHD/OX KT22 ... 9 E2
Bidhams Crs
  KWD/TDW/WH KT20 ... 13 G1
The Bield REIG RH2 ... 44 C1
Big Common La REDH RH1 ... 36 D3
Bilton Centre LHD/OX KT22 * ... 2 D4
Birch Av LHD/OX KT22 ... 2 D5
Birchgate Ms
  KWD/TDW/WH KT20 * ... 13 G1
Birch Gv KWD/TDW/WH KT20 ... 14 B4
Birchway REDH RH1 ... 46 B1
Birchwood Cl HORL RH6 ... 57 F2
Birchwood La CTHM CR3 ... 17 H5
Birkheads Rd REIG RH2 ... 33 G3
Blackborough Cl REIG RH2 ... 34 A4
Blackborough Rd REIG RH2 ... 34 B4
Blackbrook Rd RDKG RH5 ... 49 E1
The Blackburn GT/LBKH KT23 ... 8 A4
Blackhorse La
  KWD/TDW/WH KT20 ... 24 D4
Blacklands Meadow REDH RH1 ... 36 A3
Blacksmith Cl ASHTD KT21 ... 4 B4

Blackstone Cl REDH RH1 ... 34 C5
Blackstone Hl REDH RH1 ... 34 C4
Blackthorn Cl REIG RH2 ... 45 E1
Blackthorne Rd GT/LBKH KT23 ... 19 E1
Blackthorn Rd REIG RH2 ... 45 E1
Blades Cl LHD/OX KT22 ... 3 H5
Blandford Ms REIG RH2 ... 34 B4
Blanford Rd REIG RH2 ... 34 A5
Bletchingley Cl REDH RH1 ... 26 C4
Bletchingley Rd REDH RH1 ... 26 C4
Blue Leaves Av COUL/CHIP CR5 ... 16 D2
Blundell Av HORL RH6 ... 56 D3
Boleyn Wk LHD/OX KT22 ... 2 D5
Bolsover Gv REDH RH1 ... 27 E4
Bolters La BNSTD SM7 ... 7 G1
Bolters Rd HORL RH6 ... 57 E1
Bolters Rd South HORL RH6 ... 56 D1
Bond's La RDKG RH5 ... 48 B2
Bonehurst Rd HORL RH6 ... 54 A4
Bonnys Rd REIG RH2 ... 32 D4
Bonsor Dr KWD/TDW/WH KT20 ... 14 A2
Bookham Ct GT/LBKH KT23 ... 8 B3
Bookham Gv GT/LBKH KT23 ... 18 D1
The Borough
  BRKHM/BTCW RH3 ... 30 C5
Boterys Cross REDH RH1 ... 36 D3
Bourne Gv ASHTD KT21 ... 3 H4
Bourne Rd REDH RH1 ... 26 C5
Bowen Wy COUL/CHIP CR5 ... 16 D2
Bower Hill Cl REDH RH1 ... 47 E1
Bower Hill La REDH RH1 ... 35 H5
Bowyers Cl ASHTD KT21 ... 4 B3
Boxhill Rd DORK RH4 ... 30 A2
  KWD/TDW/WH KT20 ... 22 B5
Boxhill Wy BRKHM/BTCW RH3 ... 41 H1
Box Tree Wk REDH RH1 ... 45 E2
Bracken Cl GT/LBKH KT23 ... 8 B4
Bradley La RDKG RH5 ... 29 F2
Braes Md REDH RH1 ... 36 A5
Brakey Hl REDH RH1 ... 37 G4
Bramble Cl REDH RH1 ... 46 A1
Bramblehall La
  KWD/TDW/WH KT20 ... 30 B2
Bramble Hall La
  KWD/TDW/WH KT20 * ... 30 B2
Brambletye Park Rd REDH RH1 ... 45 H1
Bramble Wk REDH RH1 * ... 46 A1
Bramblewood REDH RH1 ... 26 B4
Bramley Cl REDH RH1 ... 45 G1
Bramley Gv ASHTD KT21 ... 3 H4
Bramley Wk HORL RH6 ... 57 G3
Bramley Wy ASHTD KT21 ... 4 B2
Brandsland REIG RH2 ... 44 D3
Breech La KWD/TDW/WH KT20 ... 13 E5
Bremner Av HORL RH6 ... 56 D2
Brewer St REDH RH1 ... 37 E1
Brew House Rd
  BRKHM/BTCW RH3 ... 41 H3
Briars Wd HORL RH6 ... 57 G2
Brickfield La HORL RH6 ... 56 B5
Bridges Cl HORL RH6 ... 57 H3
Bridge St LHD/OX KT22 ... 10 A2
Brier Lea KWD/TDW/WH KT20 ... 24 B4
Brier Rd KWD/TDW/WH KT20 ... 6 B4
Brightlands Rd REIG RH2 ... 34 A2
Brighton Rd COUL/CHIP CR5 ... 16 B1
  HORL RH6 ... 56 D3
  KWD/TDW/WH KT20 ... 7 E3
  KWD/TDW/WH KT20 ... 24 C2
  REDH RH1 ... 54 A2
Brighton Ter REDH RH1 ... 34 D5
The Brindles BNSTD SM7 ... 7 F2
Broadfield Cl
  KWD/TDW/WH KT20 ... 6 C5
Broadhurst ASHTD KT21 ... 4 A1
Broadhurst Gdns REIG RH2 ... 44 D2
Broadlands HORL RH6 ... 57 G2
Broadmead ASHTD KT21 ... 4 A3
  HORL RH6 ... 57 G2
  REDH RH1 * ... 26 C3
Broad Wk COUL/CHIP CR5 ... 16 A2
  EPSOM KT18 ... 6 C4

Broadwood Rd COUL/CHIP CR5 ...16 D1
Brockham Hill Pk
  KWD/TDW/WH KT20......................31 E1
Brockhamhurst Rd
  BRKHM/BTCW RH3......................49 H1
Brockham La
  BRKHM/BTCW RH3......................30 C4
Brodrick Gv GT/LBKH KT23 ....18 C1
Brokes Crs REIG RH2 ....33 G2
Brokes Rd REIG RH2 ....33 G2
Brook Cl DORK RH4.......................29 G4
Brookers Cl ASHTD KT21................3 C1
Brookfield Cl ASHTD KT21...............4 A5
  REDH RH1..................................46 A5
Brooklands Wy REDH RH1.............34 C2
Brook Rd REDH RH1......................34 D5
Brookside RDKG RH5.....................49 F5
Brook Va RDKG RH5.......................48 B2
Brook Wy LHD/OX KT22...................3 E3
Brookwood Hill REDH RH1.............57 F2
Brookwood Pk HORL RH6 ....57 F4
Broome Cl EPSOM KT18..................22 B1
Broomfield Pk DORK RH4...............39 E2
Broomhurst Ct DORK RH4..............40 B3
Browning Rd LHD/OX KT22.............9 F5
Brownlow Rd REDH RH1.................34 C4
The Brow REDH RH1......................46 A4
Brympton Cl DORK RH4..................40 A3
Buckhurst Cl REDH RH1.................34 C2
Buckingham Rd RDKG RH5.............48 C5
Buckland La BRKHM/BTCW RH3...23 F5
  BRKHM/BTCW RH3......................32 B1
Buckland Rd
  KWD/TDW/WH KT20......................24 B4
  REIG RH2.....................................32 D3
Buckles Wy BNSTD SM7..................7 E1
Budgen Dr REDH RH1....................35 E1
Buffers La LHD/OX KT22...................3 E4
Bullfinch Cl HORL RH6....................56 C2
Bull Hl LHD/OX KT22......................10 A1
Bunbury Wy EW KT17.......................6 B1
Bunce Common Rd REIG RH2.......50 C1
Burgh Heath Rd EW KT17.................6 A1
Burlington Pl REIG RH2..................33 G3
Burney Cl LHD/OX KT22...................9 E5
Burney Rd RDKG RH5.....................29 E1
Burnham Dr REIG RH2....................33 G3
Burnhams Rd GT/LBKH KT23..........8 B4
Burnside ASHTD KT21......................4 B3
The Burrell DORK RH4...................39 E2
Burrows Cl GT/LBKH KT23..............8 B4
Burton Cl HORL RH6.......................57 E4
Burwood Cl REIG RH2....................34 B4
Bushbury La
  BRKHM/BTCW RH3......................41 G1
Bushetts Gv REDH RH1.................26 B4
Bushfield Dr REDH RH1..................46 A4
Bushy Rd LHD/OX KT22....................8 D2
Bushy Shaw ASHTD KT21................3 G2
Butter Hl DORK RH4........................40 A1
Byron Pl LHD/OX KT22...................10 B2
Byttom Hl RDKG RH5......................20 C2

C

Caberfeigh Cl REDH RH1...............34 C4
Caberfeigh Pl REDH RH1 *..............34 B4
Caen Wood Rd ASHTD KT21............3 C3
Cage Yd REIG RH2 *.......................33 G4
Calvert Crs DORK RH4....................29 F4
Calvert Rd DORK RH4....................29 F4
Cambridge Lodge Pk
  HORL RH6...................................54 A5
Cambridge Sq REDH RH1..............46 A2
Camilla Cl GT/LBKH KT23................8 D5
Camilla Dr RDKG RH5....................20 A5
Campion Dr
  KWD/TDW/WH KT20......................6 B5
Canada Av REDH RH1....................46 A3
Canada Dr REDH RH1....................46 A3
Candy Cft GT/LBKH KT23...............18 D1
Can Hatch KWD/TDW/WH KT20........7 E3
Cannon Gv LHD/OX KT22.................9 E2
Cannon Side LHD/OX KT22..............9 E2
Cannon Wy LHD/OX KT22................9 E2
Canons Cl REIG RH2......................33 F3
Canons La KWD/TDW/WH KT20........7 E4
Canterbury Ct DORK RH4 *............29 E5
Carlton Ct HORL RH6 *...................57 F1
Carlton Gn REDH RH1....................34 B4
Carlton Rd REIG RH2......................34 B2
Carlton Tye HORL RH6...................57 H3
Carrington Cl REDH RH1................34 B1
Cartersmead Cl HORL RH6............57 F2
Cartmel Cl REDH RH1....................34 C3
Castle Cl REDH RH1.......................37 E3
  REIG RH2....................................44 D3

Castle Dr HORL RH6......................57 G5
  REIG RH2....................................44 C3
Castlefield Rd REIG RH2................33 G3
Castle Gdns DORK RH4..................30 B4
Castle Sq REDH RH1......................37 E3
Castle St REDH RH1.......................36 D3
Cavendish Gdns REDH RH1...........35 E4
Cavendish Rd REDH RH1...............35 E4
Caxton Ri REDH RH1......................35 E3
Cayton Rd COUL/CHIP CR5.............16 D2
Cedar Cl DORK RH4.......................40 B1
Cedar Dr LHD/OX KT22....................9 G3
The Cedars BRKHM/BTCW RH3....30 C4
  LHD/OX KT22..............................10 D1
  REIG RH2....................................34 B4
Cedar Wk KWD/TDW/WH KT20......14 B1
Central Pde REDH RH6 *..................5 F3
Chadhurst Cl RDKG RH5................40 D4
Chaffers Md ASHTD KT21.................4 B4
Chaffinch Wy HORL RH6.................56 C2
Chaldon Cl REDH RH1....................45 G1
Chalk La ASHTD KT21......................4 C4
  EPSOM KT18...............................5 E4
Chalkpit La BRKHM/BTCW RH3....30 D3
  DORK RH4..................................29 E4
Chalk Pit La GT/LBKH KT23...........18 B2
Chalk Pit Rd BNSTD SM7.................7 G2
  EPSOM KT18...............................5 E4
Chalkpit Ter DORK RH4..................29 E4
Challenge Ct LHD/OX KT22..............3 F4
Champion Down EHSLY KT24.........18 A3
Chanctonbury Cha REDH RH1......35 F5
Chantrey Cl ASHTD KT21.................3 G4
Chantry Cl HORL RH6....................56 D2
Chapel Ct DORK RH4 *...................40 A1
Chapel Gv EPSOM KT18...................6 D5
Chapel La DORK RH4.....................39 E2
  GT/LBKH KT23............................19 E3
Chapel Rd KWD/TDW/WH KT20......13 G3
  REDH RH1...................................34 D4
Chapel Wk COUL/CHIP CR5............16 D2
Chapel Wy EPSOM KT18...................6 C4
Charlesfield Rd HORL RH6.............56 D4
Charlwood Cl GT/LBKH KT23...........8 D4
Charlwood Pl REIG RH2..................33 F4
Charman Rd REDH RH1.................34 C4
Charm Cl HORL RH6......................56 C2
Chart Cl RDKG RH5........................40 C3
Chart Downs RDKG RH5.................40 C3
Chartfield Rd REIG RH2..................34 A5
Chart Gdns RDKG RH5...................40 C3
Chart La DORK RH4........................40 B1
  REIG RH2....................................33 H4
Chart La South RDKG RH5.............40 C4
Chartway REIG RH2........................33 H4
Chartwood Pl DORK RH4................40 A1
The Chase ASHTD KT21...................3 C3
  KWD/TDW/WH KT20......................15 E1
  REDH RH1...................................34 B5
Chatelet Cl HORL RH6...................57 F2
Chave Cft EPSOM KT18 *.................6 C4
Chavecroft Ter EPSOM KT18 *........6 C4
Cheam Cl KWD/TDW/WH KT20......13 F1
Chequers Cl HORL RH6..................57 E2
  KWD/TDW/WH KT20......................13 E5
Chequers Dr HORL RH6.................57 E2
Chequers La
  KWD/TDW/WH KT20......................13 E5
Chequers Pl DORK RH4.................40 B1
Cherkley LHD/OX KT22 *.................20 D1
Cherkley Hl LHD/OX KT22..............20 C1
Cherry Green Cl REDH RH1...........46 B1
Cherry Orch ASHTD KT21................4 D3
Cherry Trees COUL/CHIP CR5.......16 D1
Chesham Rd
  KWD/TDW/WH KT20......................24 B1
Chester Cl DORK RH4....................29 G4
Chesters HORL RH6.......................56 C1
Chesterton Dr REDH RH1..............27 E3
Chestnut Cl
  KWD/TDW/WH KT20......................14 C3
  REDH RH1...................................46 B1
Chestnut Md REDH RH1.................34 C3
Chestnut Pl ASHTD KT21..................4 A4
Chestnut Rd HORL RH6..................57 E3
Chetwode Dr EPSOM KT18...............6 D3
Chetwode Rd EPSOM KT18..............6 C4
Chevington Vls REDH RH1.............37 H3
Cheyne Wk HORL RH6....................56 D5
Chichester Cl DORK RH4................29 F4
Chichester Rd DORK RH4...............29 F4
Chilberton Dr REDH RH1................26 C5
Childs Hall Dr GT/LBKH KT23..........8 B5
Childs Hall Rd GT/LBKH KT23........18 B1
Chilmans Dr GT/LBKH KT23............8 D5
Chilmark Gdns REDH RH1..............27 E4
Chilmead Rd REDH RH1 *..............34 D4
Chilmead La REDH RH1.................35 H2

The Chine DORK RH4.....................29 F5
Chipstead Cl REDH RH1.................34 D5
Chipstead La COUL/CHIP CR5........14 D4
Chipstead Rd BNSTD SM7...............7 F2
Christie Cl GT/LBKH KT23................8 B5
Chrystie La GT/LBKH KT23.............18 D1
Chuck's La KWD/TDW/WH KT20.....13 F4
Church Cl KWD/TDW/WH KT20......24 B2
  LHD/OX KT22................................9 F4
Church Ct REIG RH2.......................33 H4
Churchfield Rd REIG RH2...............33 F3
Church Gdns LHD/OX KT22 *...........3 F5
Church Gn
  KWD/TDW/WH KT20 *...................13 E4
Church Hl REDH RH1......................36 B3
Churchill Cl LHD/OX KT22................9 G3
Church La COUL/CHIP CR5.............16 A2
  CTHM CR3...................................17 G3
  EPSOM KT18...............................12 A5
  KWD/TDW/WH KT20......................6 D2
  REDH RH1...................................37 F5
Church Lane Av COUL/CHIP CR5...16 B2
Church Lane Dr COUL/CHIP CR5...16 B2
Church Rd ASHTD KT21...................3 H3
  GT/LBKH KT23..............................8 B3
  HORL RH6...................................56 D4
  LHD/OX KT22..............................10 B2
  REDH RH1...................................45 G1
  REIG RH2....................................44 C1
Church St BRKHM/BTCW RH3.......31 G5
  DORK RH4..................................40 A1
  LHD/OX KT22..............................10 B2
  REIG RH2....................................33 H4
Church Ter RDKG RH5 *..................48 C5
Church View Cl HORL RH6..............56 D4
Church Wk HORL RH6....................56 D4
  REIG RH2....................................33 H4
The Circus LHD/OX KT22 *...............3 F5
Clare Crs LHD/OX KT22....................3 E3
Claremont Ct DORK RH4.................40 B2
Claremont Rd REDH RH1...............35 E1
Claremount Cl EPSOM KT18............6 C2
Claremount Gdns EPSOM KT18.......6 D2
Clarence Ct HORL RH6...................57 H3
Clarence Rd REDH RH1..................45 F2
Clarence Wk REDH RH1..................45 F2
Clarence Wy HORL RH6..................57 H3
Clarendon Ms ASHTD KT21.............4 A4
Clarendon Rd REDH RH1................34 D3
Clare Wd LHD/OX KT22....................3 E3
Claygate Rd DORK RH4..................40 B3
Clayhall La REIG RH2......................44 A2
Clayhill Cl REIG RH2.......................51 E1
Clayhill Rd REIG RH2......................50 D2
Clay La EPSOM KT18.......................11 H4
  REDH RH1...................................35 G5
Cleardene DORK RH4.....................40 B1
The Clears REIG RH2......................33 E2
Cleeve Rd LHD/OX KT22...................3 E5
Clerks Cft REDH RH1......................37 F3
Clifton Cl HORL RH6.......................57 H3
Clifton's La REIG RH2.....................32 D3
Clifton Ter DORK RH4 *...................40 B2
Cliftonville DORK RH4.....................40 B2
Clinton Rd LHD/OX KT22.................10 C3
The Close BRKHM/BTCW RH3.......41 H3
  HORL RH6...................................57 G5
  REIG RH2....................................33 H5
Cloverfields HORL RH6...................57 F2
Clover Hl COUL/CHIP CR5..............16 B3
Clump Av KWD/TDW/WH KT20.......31 E1
Clyde Cl REDH RH1.........................35 E3
Coach House Ms REDH RH1..........34 D5
Coach Rd BRKHM/BTCW RH3.......41 G1
  DORK RH4..................................30 A4
Coast Hl DORK RH4........................38 B3
Coast Hill La DORK RH4.................38 C3
Cock La LHD/OX KT22......................9 E2
Cockshot Hl REIG RH2....................44 D1
Cockshot Rd REIG RH2...................44 D1
Colcokes Rd BNSTD SM7.................7 G1
Coldharbour La DORK RH4............40 A3
  REDH RH1...................................37 H4
Colebrooke Rd REDH RH1.............34 C2
Colesmead Rd REDH RH1..............34 D1
College Crs REDH RH1...................35 E1
Colley La REIG RH2........................33 E3
Colley Manor Dr REIG RH2.............32 D3
Colley Wy REIG RH2.......................33 E1
Collingwood Cl HORL RH6..............57 F2
Colman Cl EPSOM KT18...................6 C2
Colman Wy REDH RH1...................34 C2
Common Rd REDH RH1..................45 H1
Commonside GT/LBKH KT23............8 C3
Coneyberry REIG RH2.....................45 E3
Coneybury REDH RH1.....................37 G4
Conifer Cl REIG RH2.......................33 G2
Coniston Wy REIG RH2...................34 C3
Consort Wy HORL RH6...................57 E3

Consort Wy East HORL RH6..........57 F[?]
The Coombe
  BRKHM/BTCW RH3......................31 F
Cooper's Hill Rd REDH RH1...........47 H
Copleigh Dr
  KWD/TDW/WH KT20......................7 E
Copley Cl REDH RH1......................34 C
Copley Wy
  KWD/TDW/WH KT20......................6 D
Copperfields LHD/OX KT22..............9 E
Coppice La REIG RH2......................33 E
Copse La HORL RH6.......................57 H
Copse Rd REIG RH2........................45 E
The Copse LHD/OX KT22..................8 D
  REDH RH1...................................47 E
Copsleigh Av REDH RH1................54 A
Copsleigh Cl REDH RH1.................46 A
Copsleigh Wy REDH RH1................46 A
Copt Hill La
  KWD/TDW/WH KT20......................7 E
Copthorne Ct LHD/OX KT22 *.........10 A
Copthorne Rd LHD/OX KT22............3 E
Corfe Cl ASHTD KT21.......................3 F
Cormongers La REDH RH1.............35 H
Corner Farm Cl
  KWD/TDW/WH KT20......................13 E
Cornfield Rd REIG RH2...................34 A
The Coronet HORL RH6..................57 H
Cotland Acres REDH RH1...............45 E
Courtlands Crs BNSTD SM7.............7 F
Court Lodge Rd HORL RH6.............56 C
Cowslip La RDKG RH5.....................20 B
Coxdean EPSOM KT18......................6 C
Crab Hill La REDH RH1...................35 H
Crabtree Cl GT/LBKH KT23.............19 E
Crabtree Dr LHD/OX KT22...............3 F
Crabtree La EPSOM KT18...............22 B
  GT/LBKH KT23............................19 E
  RDKG RH5...................................19 E
Craddocks Av ASHTD KT21..............4 A
  EPSOM KT18...............................11 H
Craddock's Cl ASHTD KT21.............3 H
Cradhurst Cl DORK RH4..................39 E
Crakell Rd REIG RH2.......................34 A
Crampshaw La ASHTD KT21............4 C
Cranbourne Cl HORL RH6 *............57 E
Cranston Cl REIG RH2....................33 E
Cray Av ASHTD KT21.........................4 B
Crescent Ct HORL RH6 *................57 H
Crescent Rd REDH RH1..................37 E
  REIG RH2....................................44 C
The Crescent HORL RH6.................57 H
  LHD/OX KT22..............................10 C
  REDH RH1 *................................45 E
  REIG RH2....................................33 E
Crescent Wy HORL RH6..................57 F
Cressall Cl LHD/OX KT22..................3 E
Cressall Md LHD/OX KT22................3 E
Crewdson Rd HORL RH6.................57 E
Cricket Rd REDH RH1.....................47 E
Croffets KWD/TDW/WH KT20..........14 B
Croft Av DORK RH4.........................29 E
Crofters Cl REDH RH1....................46 A
Crofton ASHTD KT21.........................4 B
Cromwell Rd REDH RH1.................34 D
Cronks Hl REIG RH2........................34 B
Cronks Hill Cl REDH RH1................46 A
Cronks Hill Rd REDH RH1...............46 A
Crossland Rd REDH RH1................34 C
Cross Oak La REDH RH1.................55 E
Cross Rd KWD/TDW/WH KT20........14 A
Crossways La REIG RH2..................25 E
The Crossways REDH RH1..............45 H
Croydon Rd REIG RH2....................44 A
Crutchfield La HORL RH6...............55 F
Cuddington Cl
  KWD/TDW/WH KT20......................6 C
Culverhay ASHTD KT21.....................4 A
Cunliffe Cl EPSOM KT18..................11 F
Curtis Rd DORK RH4.......................39 E
Cygnets Cl REDH RH1.....................35 E

D

Dale Vw EPSOM KT18.......................5 G
Daneshill REDH RH1.......................46 A
Daneshill Cl REDH RH1...................46 A
Darcy Pl ASHTD KT21........................4 B
Darcy Rd ASHTD KT21.......................4 B
Darenth Wy HORL RH6....................55 H
Dawnay Rd GT/LBKH KT23...............8 B
Daymerslea Rdg
  LHD/OX KT22..............................10 D
Dayseys Hl REDH RH1....................55 F
Dean La REDH RH1.........................25 F
Deanoak La REIG RH2....................43 G
Deans Cl KWD/TDW/WH KT20........14 C

Deans La KWD/TDW/WH KT20......**13** F5
  REDH RH1......................................**36** C3
Deans Rd REDH RH1........................**26** C5
Dean Wk GT/LBKH KT23.............**18** D1
De Burgh Gdns
  KWD/TDW/WH KT20.................**6** D4
De Burgh Pk BNSTD SM7..............**7** H1
Deepdene Av RDKG RH5..............**40** C1
Deepdene Avenue Rd
  DORK RH4..................................**29** G4
Deepdene Dr RDKG RH5...............**40** C1
Deepdene Gdns DORK RH4..........**29** H5
Deepdene Park Rd RDKG RH5......**29** H5
  RDKG RH5..................................**40** C1
Deepdene V DORK RH4..................**29** G4
Deepdene Wd RDKG RH5...............**40** D1
Deepfields HORL RH6......................**56** D1
Deerings Rd REIG RH2...................**33** H4
Deerleap Rd DORK RH4..................**38** D2
Delabole Rd REDH RH1..................**27** E4
Delamere Rd REIG RH2..................**44** D3
Delderfield ASHTD KT21..................**3** H5
Dell Cl LHD/OX KT22........................**9** F3
  RDKG RH5..................................**20** C2
The Dell HORL RH6.........................**56** A1
  HORL RH6...................................**57** F2
  KWD/TDW/WH KT20.................**13** C1
  REIG RH2.....................................**33** C3
Delta Dr HORL RH6.........................**57** E5
Delves KWD/TDW/WH KT20.........**13** H1
Dene Cl HORL RH6...........................**56** C1
Dene Rd ASHTD KT21.......................**4** B4
Dene St DORK RH4...........................**40** H1
Dene Street Gdns DORK RH4.......**40** B1
Denfield DORK RH4..........................**40** B3
Dennis Cl REDH RH1.......................**34** C2
Denton Cl REDH RH1......................**46** A4
Dents Gv KWD/TDW/WH KT20......**24** B3
Derby Arms Rd EPSOM KT18..........**5** H2
Derby Cl EPSOM KT18.......................**6** B4
Derby Stables Rd EPSOM KT18.......**5** C2
Devitt Cl ASHTD KT21.......................**4** C1
Devon Cres REDH RH1....................**34** B4
Devon Rd REDH RH1.......................**26** C5
Devonshire Av
  KWD/TDW/WH KT20.................**31** E1
Dinsdale Cl BNSTD SM7...................**7** F1
Dingleston Rd LHD/OX KT22.............**3** E4
Doctors La CTHM CR3....................**17** G4
Dodds Pk BRKHM/BTCW RH3......**41** H1
Dome Wy REDH RH1......................**34** D3
Dorincourt Gdns REIG RH2...........**33** H3
Dods Pl REIG RH2 *.........................**34** A3
Dods Rd REIG RH2...........................**34** A3
Dods Wy REIG RH2.........................**34** B3
Doran Dr REDH RH1.......................**34** B4
Doran Gdns REDH RH1 *...............**34** B4
Dorking Rd KWD/TDW/WH KT20...**7** F5
Dorking Rd GT/LBKH KT23............**18** D2
  KWD/TDW/WH KT20.................**22** D3
  LHD/OX KT22.............................**10** B5
Douglas Ms BNSTD SM7..................**7** F1
Douglas Rd REIG RH2....................**33** G3
Dovers Green Rd REIG RH2...........**44** D4
Dowlans Cl GT/LBKH KT23............**18** C2
Dowlans Rd GT/LBKH KT23...........**18** D2
Downe Cl HORL RH6.......................**56** C1
Downland Cl EPSOM KT18...............**6** B3
Downland Gdns EPSOM KT18..........**6** B3
Downland Wy EPSOM KT18.............**6** B3
Downs Ct LHD/OX KT22.................**10** B3
Downs Rd EPSOM KT18....................**5** E5
  RDKG RH5..................................**20** C3
The Downs LHD/OX KT22..............**10** C5
Downs Vw DORK RH4.....................**29** G4
  KWD/TDW/WH KT20.................**13** F1
Downsview Gdns DORK RH4.........**40** B2
Downs View Rd GT/LBKH KT23....**19** E2
Downs Wy EPSOM KT18...................**5** H1
  GT/LBKH KT23...........................**19** E1
  KWD/TDW/WH KT20.................**13** F1
Downsway Cl
  KWD/TDW/WH KT20.................**13** C1
Downs Wd EPSOM KT18...................**6** B3
Dragswood REIG RH2.....................**34** B2
Drake Rd HORL RH6........................**56** C3
Drakston Cl LHD/OX KT22..............**9** G3
Driftway LHD/OX KT22...................**10** C3
Dixon Sp KWD/TDW/WH KT20......**14** D1
Drive BNSTD SM7...............................**7** E2
  HORL RH6...................................**57** F5
  LHD/OX KT22 *...........................**14** C4
  LHD/OX KT22................................**9** C2
  LHD/OX KT22.............................**11** E3
Druids Cl ASHTD KT21......................**4** B5
Druid Rd
  KWD/TDW/WH KT20.................**13** F4
Druids Ride RDKG RH5..................**40** D4
Drungeon Rd KWD/TDW/WH KT20...**7** E4

Duncroft Cl REIG RH2.....................**33** F4
Dundrey Crs REDH RH1.................**27** E4
Dungates La
  BRKHM/BTCW RH3..................**41** H3
Dunlin Cl REDH RH1.......................**45** G4
Dunottar Cl REDH RH1...................**45** F1
Dunraven Av REDH RH1.................**54** B2
Durfold Dr REIG RH2......................**34** A4
Durleston Park Dr GT/LBKH KT23..**9** E5
Duxhurst La REIG RH2...................**52** D4
Dyson Ct DORK RH4 *....................**40** A1

E

Earlsbrook Rd REDH RH1..............**45** H1
Earlswood Rd REDH RH1...............**45** H1
Eastfield Rd REDH RH1..................**46** C1
Eastnor Pl REIG RH2 *....................**44** C1
Eastnor Rd REIG RH2....................**44** C1
East Rd REIG RH2...........................**33** F3
East St GT/LBKH KT23.....................**8** D5
East Wk REIG RH2..........................**33** H4
Eastwick Dr GT/LBKH KT23.............**8** D4
Eastwick Park Av GT/LBKH KT23...**8** D5
Eastwick Rd GT/LBKH KT23.............**8** D5
Ebbisham Cl DORK RH4.................**40** A1
Ebbisham La
  KWD/TDW/WH KT20.................**12** D1
Eccles Hl RDKG RH5......................**40** C5
Edenside Rd GT/LBKH KT23............**8** A4
Edes Cottages ASHTD KT21 *..........**3** H4
Edgefield Cl REDH RH1..................**46** A4
Edgeley GT/LBKH KT23....................**8** A4
Effingham Rd REIG RH2.................**33** H5
Egmont Park Rd
  KWD/TDW/WH KT20.................**13** E5
Egmont Wy KWD/TDW/WH KT20....**7** H4
Eighth Av KWD/TDW/WH KT20 *...**24** B1
Eldersley Cl REDH RH1..................**34** D2
Eldersley Gdns REDH RH1............**34** D2
Elder Wy RDKG RH5.......................**40** C5
Eleventh Av
  KWD/TDW/WH KT20 *..............**24** B1
Elizabeth Ct HORL RH6 *..............**57** E3
Ellington Wy EPSOM KT18...............**6** B2
Elm Cl KWD/TDW/WH KT20...........**22** A5
  LHD/OX KT22.............................**10** B2
Elmcroft GT/LBKH KT23 *................**8** C3
Elm Dr LHD/OX KT22......................**10** B2
Elmer Cottages LHD/OX KT22 *....**10** A3
Elmer Ms LHD/OX KT22.................**10** A3
Elmfield GT/LBKH KT23....................**8** C3
Elm Gdns EPSOM KT18.....................**6** C4
Elmhurst Dr DORK RH4..................**40** B3
Elmore Rd COUL/CHIP CR5...........**15** H1
Elm Rd LHD/OX KT22......................**10** B2
  REDH RH1..................................**34** C1
Elmshorn EW KT17...........................**6** C1
Elmswood GT/LBKH KT23................**8** B1
Elm Tree Cl HORL RH6 *...............**57** E2
Elmwood Ct ASHTD KT21.................**3** H2
Elmwood Rd REDH RH1.................**26** A5
Emerton Rd LHD/OX KT22................**2** C1
Emily Davison Dr EPSOM KT18......**6** B3
Emlyn La LHD/OX KT22...................**10** A2
Emlyn Rd HORL RH6.......................**56** C2
  REDH RH1..................................**46** A1
Empire Vls REDH RH1....................**54** A4
Endsleigh REDH RH1......................**26** C4
Epsom La North EPSOM KT18..........**6** B4
Epsom La South
  KWD/TDW/WH KT20.................**13** G2
Epsom Rd ASHTD KT21....................**4** B3
  LHD/OX KT22.............................**10** B1
Ermyn Cl LHD/OX KT22..................**10** D1
Ermyn Wy LHD/OX KT22................**10** D1
Eversfield Rd REIG RH2.................**33** H4
Evesham Cl REIG RH2....................**33** F3
Evesham Rd REIG RH2...................**33** F3
Evesham Rd North REIG RH2........**33** F3
Ewelands HORL RH6.......................**57** G2
Ewood La RDKG RH5......................**49** F5
Eyhurst Cl KWD/TDW/WH KT20....**14** B4
Eyhurst Pk
  KWD/TDW/WH KT20 *..............**15** E3
Eyhurst Sp KWD/TDW/WH KT20....**14** B4

F

The Facade REIG RH2....................**33** G3
Fairacres KWD/TDW/WH KT20.....**13** G1
Fairfax Av REDH RH1......................**34** D3
Fairfield Av HORL RH6....................**57** E5
Fairfield Cl GT/LBKH KT23...............**8** D5
Fairfield Dr DORK RH4....................**29** F4

Fairfield Rd LHD/OX KT22..............**10** B1
Fairfield Wk LHD/OX KT22.............**10** B1
Fairford Cl REIG RH2.....................**34** A2
Fairhaven Rd REDH RH1................**26** A5
Fairholme Crs ASHTD KT21.............**3** G2
Fair La COUL/CHIP CR5.................**15** E5
Fairlawn GT/LBKH KT23....................**8** B4
Fairlawn Dr REDH RH1...................**45** G1
Fairlawns HORL RH6.......................**57** F4
Fairstone Ct HORL RH6..................**57** F2
The Fairways REDH RH1................**45** F2
The Fairway HORL RH6....................**3** C3
Falcon Wd LHD/OX KT22..................**2** D5
Falkland Gv DORK RH4..................**40** A2
Falkland Rd DORK RH4..................**40** A2
Fallowfield Wy HORL RH6..............**57** F2
Farm Cl LHD/OX KT22......................**9** F4
Farm La ASHTD KT21........................**4** A5
Felland Wy REIG RH2.....................**45** F3
Feltham Rd REDH RH1...................**45** H4
Fengates Rd REDH RH1.................**34** C4
Fenton Cl REDH RH1......................**35** E4
Fenton Rd REDH RH1.....................**35** E4
Ferndale Rd BNSTD SM7..................**7** F1
Fernham Rd HORL RH6...................**57** E1
Fernlea GT/LBKH KT23......................**8** D4
Ferriers Wy EPSOM KT18................**6** C4
Fetcham Common La
  LHD/OX KT22................................**8** D1
Fetcham Park Dr
  LHD/OX KT22................................**9** G3
The Fieldings BNSTD SM7................**7** F2
  HORL RH6...................................**57** F2
Fieldview HORL RH6........................**57** F2
Fife Wy GT/LBKH KT23.....................**8** C5
Fifteenth Av
  KWD/TDW/WH KT20 *..............**24** B1
Fifth Av
  KWD/TDW/WH KT20 *..............**24** B1
Figgswood COUL/CHIP CR5...........**16** C2
Fiona Cl GT/LBKH KT23....................**8** C4
Firlands HORL RH6..........................**57** F2
Firs Cl DORK RH4............................**40** A3
First Av KWD/TDW/WH KT20 *.......**24** B1
The Firs GT/LBKH KT23....................**8** D5
Fir Tree Cl LHD/OX KT22................**10** C3
Fir Tree Rd EW KT17.........................**6** B1
  LHD/OX KT22.............................**10** C3
Fir Tree Wk REIG RH2....................**34** B4
Fitzroy Pl REIG RH2........................**34** B4
Flanchford Rd REIG RH2................**43** G4
Fleetwood Cl
  KWD/TDW/WH KT20.................**13** H1
Flint Cl GT/LBKH KT23....................**19** E1
  REDH RH1..................................**34** D3
Flint Cottages
  LHD/OX KT22 *...........................**10** B1
Flint Hl DORK RH4..........................**40** B3
Flint Hill Cl DORK RH4...................**40** B4
Folly La RDKG RH5.........................**48** B4
Forest Crs ASHTD KT21....................**4** C1
Forest Dr
  KWD/TDW/WH KT20.................**14** C1
Forest Wy ASHTD KT21.....................**4** C2
Forge Bridge La
  COUL/CHIP CR5.......................**16** B2
Forge Pl HORL RH6.........................**56** C5
Fort La REIG RH2............................**24** D5
Fort Rd KWD/TDW/WH KT20.........**30** D1
Fortyfoot Rd LHD/OX KT22............**10** D2
Fountain Rd REDH RH1..................**45** G1
Fourteenth Av
  KWD/TDW/WH KT20 *..............**24** B1
Fourth Av
  KWD/TDW/WH KT20 *..............**24** B1
Fox Covert LHD/OX KT22..................**9** F4
Fox La GT/LBKH KT23........................**8** B4
Foxley Rd REDH RH1......................**33** H1
Foxley Cl REDH RH1.......................**46** A4
Frenches Rd REDH RH1.................**35** F1
The Frenches REDH RH1...............**35** E2
Frensham Wy EW KT17.....................**6** C1
Freshfield Flats
  KWD/TDW/WH KT20 *..............**24** B2
Friars Orch LHD/OX KT22.................**9** F1
Friths Dr REIG RH2.........................**33** H1
Fuel Farm Rd HORL RH6................**56** C5
Fulbourne Cl REDH RH1.................**34** C2
Fullers Wood La REDH RH1...........**35** G4
Furlong Rd DORK RH4....................**39** G2
Furze Cl HORL RH6.........................**57** H3
  REDH RH1..................................**34** D3
Furzefield Crs REIG RH2................**45** E1
Furzefield Rd REIG RH2.................**45** E1
Furze Gv KWD/TDW/WH KT20.......**14** D1
Furze Hl KWD/TDW/WH KT20........**14** B1
Furzehill REDH RH1........................**34** C3
Furze Pl REDH RH1 *......................**34** D3

G

The Gables BNSTD SM7...................**7** F2
Gables Wy BNSTD SM7....................**7** F1
Gadbrook Rd
  BRKHM/BTCW RH3..................**42** B5
Gale Crs BNSTD SM7.......................**7** G2
Garden Cl LHD/OX KT22.................**10** C4
Gardener's Wk GT/LBKH KT23.......**18** D1
Garden Wk COUL/CHIP CR5..........**16** B3
Garibaldi Rd REDH RH1.................**34** D5
Garlands Rd LHD/OX KT22.............**10** B1
  REDH RH1..................................**34** D4
Garlichill Rd EPSOM KT18...............**6** B2
Garrard Rd BNSTD SM7...................**7** C1
Garratts La BNSTD SM7...................**7** F1
The Garstons GT/LBKH KT23...........**8** B5
Gatehouse Ldg REDH RH1.............**46** A2
Gatesden Cl LHD/OX KT22...............**9** E3
Gatesden Rd LHD/OX KT22..............**9** E3
Gatton Bottom REIG RH2...............**25** H3
Gatton Cl REIG RH2........................**34** A1
Gatton Park Rd REIG RH2..............**34** B1
Gatton Rd REIG RH2.......................**34** A1
Gaveston Rd LHD/OX KT22..............**3** E5
Gawton Crs COUL/CHIP CR5..........**16** C1
Gayler Cl REDH RH1.......................**37** H4
Gayton Cl ASHTD KT21.....................**4** A3
Gaywood Rd ASHTD KT21................**4** B3
Gerrards Md BNSTD SM7.................**7** F1
Gilmais GT/LBKH KT23......................**9** E5
Gimcrack Hl LHD/OX KT22.............**10** B2
Glade Sp KWD/TDW/WH KT20.......**14** D1
The Glade KWD/TDW/WH KT20.....**14** D1
  LHD/OX KT22................................**8** D2
Gladstone Rd ASHTD KT21..............**3** H3
Glebe Cl GT/LBKH KT23..................**18** C1
Glebe Rd ASHTD KT21......................**3** H3
  DORK RH4..................................**39** H1
  REDH RH1..................................**16** A4
The Glebe HORL RH6......................**56** D3
  REIG RH2...................................**51** E1
Gledhow Wd
  KWD/TDW/WH KT20.................**14** D2
Glen Cl KWD/TDW/WH KT20..........**14** D2
Glenfield Cl BRKHM/BTCW RH3....**41** H3
Glenfield Rd BRKHM/BTCW RH3...**41** H3
Glenheadon Cl LHD/OX KT22.........**10** D3
Glenheadon Ri LHD/OX KT22.........**10** D3
Glenwood RDKG RH5......................**40** C3
Glory Md DORK RH4........................**40** C4
Gloucester Rd REDH RH1..............**34** D3
Glover's Rd REIG RH2....................**33** H5
Godstone Rd REDH RH1.................**37** G3
Goldcrest Cl HORL RH6..................**56** B2
Goldstone Farm Vw
  GT/LBKH KT23...........................**18** C2
Goodwood Rd REDH RH1...............**34** D2
Goodwyns Rd DORK RH4...............**40** B4
Gordon Ct REDH RH1 *..................**45** H1
Gordon Rd REDH RH1....................**35** E1
Gorse Cl KWD/TDW/WH KT20.........**6** B5
Gower Rd HORL RH6.......................**56** C3
Granary Cl HORL RH6.....................**57** E1
Grand Stand Rd EPSOM KT18.........**5** H2
Grange Cl LHD/OX KT22....................**3** H5
  REDH RH1..................................**26** B3
  REDH RH1..................................**37** F3
Grange Dr REDH RH1.....................**26** B3
Grangemount LHD/OX KT22............**3** H5
Grange Rd LHD/OX KT22..................**3** H5
Grantwood Cl REDH RH1...............**46** A4
Grassmere HORL RH6.....................**57** F2
Gravel Hl LHD/OX KT22..................**10** A1
Gray's La ASHTD KT21......................**4** A4
Grays Wd HORL RH6.......................**57** G3
Great Ellshams BNSTD SM7.............**7** G1
Greatlake Ct HORL RH6..................**57** F2
Great Tattenhams EPSOM KT18.......**6** C4
Greenacres GT/LBKH KT23...............**8** C4
  KWD/TDW/WH KT20.................**24** B3
Greenfields Cl HORL RH6...............**56** C1
Greenfields Rd HORL RH6..............**56** C1
Greenhayes Cl REIG RH2...............**34** A4
Green La ASHTD KT21.......................**3** G2
  KWD/TDW/WH KT20.................**24** B1
  LHD/OX KT22.............................**10** D1
  REDH RH1..................................**34** C2
  REDH RH1..................................**46** A4
  REIG RH2.....................................**51** F2
  REIG RH2...................................**33** F4
Greensand Cl REDH RH1................**26** D3
Greensand Rd REDH RH1...............**35** E3
Greensand Wy
  BRKHM/BTCW RH3..................**32** A4
  DORK RH4..................................**39** G2
  RDKG RH5..................................**28** B4

REDH RH1.....36 A5
REDH RH1.....47 H1
REIG RH2.....44 B1
Greenside Dr *ASHTD* KT21.....3 F3
The Green *KWD/TDW/WH* KT20.....7 E4
 KWD/TDW/WH KT20.....13 H3
 LHD/OX KT22.....9 F4
Green Wy *REDH* RH1.....34 C2
Greenway *GT/LBKH* KT23.....8 D3
Greenways
 KWD/TDW/WH KT20.....13 E5
Greenwood Dr *REDH* RH1.....46 A4
Grendon Cl *HORL* RH6.....56 D1
Greville Cl *ASHTD* KT21.....4 A4
Greville Ct *GT/LBKH* KT23.....8 D5
Greville Park Av *ASHTD* KT21.....4 A3
Greville Park Rd *ASHTD* KT21.....4 A3
Greystones Cl *REDH* RH1.....45 F1
Greystones Dr *REIG* RH2.....34 A2
Griffin Ct *ASHTD* KT21 *.....4 A4
Griffin Wy *GT/LBKH* KT23.....18 C1
Grosvenor Cl *HORL* RH6.....57 E5
Grosvenor Ms *REIG* RH2.....44 D2
Grosvenor Rd *EPSOM* KT18.....5 G4
Grovehill Rd *REDH* RH1.....34 C4
Grove Rd *ASHTD* KT21.....4 B3
 HORL RH6.....56 C2
Grove Shaw
 KWD/TDW/WH KT20.....14 A4
Groveside *GT/LBKH* KT23.....18 C2
Groveside Cl *GT/LBKH* KT23.....18 C2
The Grove *CTHM* CR3.....17 H1
 HORL RH6.....57 F4
Guildford Rd *DORK* RH4.....38 D3
 GT/LBKH KT23.....9 F5
 GT/LBKH KT23.....18 B3
 LHD/OX KT22.....10 A2
Gurney's Cl *REDH* RH1.....34 D5

H

Haigh Crs *REDH* RH1.....46 B1
Halepit Rd *GT/LBKH* KT23.....19 E1
Hales Oak *GT/LBKH* KT23.....19 E1
Hambledon Cl *LHD/OX* KT18.....5 E1
Hambledon Pl *GT/LBKH* KT23.....8 D3
Hambledon V *EPSOM* KT18.....5 E1
Hamilton Pl
 KWD/TDW/WH KT20.....14 B3
Hampstead La *DORK* RH4.....39 H2
Hampstead Rd *DORK* RH4.....40 A2
Hampton Rd *REDH* RH1.....45 H4
Hanover Cl *REDH* RH1.....26 C3
Hanover Ct *DORK* RH4.....39 H1
Hanworth Rd *REDH* RH1.....45 H4
Harden Farm Cl
 COUL/CHIP CR5.....16 C1
Harding Rd *EPSOM* KT18.....5 G4
Hardwicke Rd *REIG* RH2.....33 G3
Hardwick Rd *REDH* RH1.....45 F1
Hardy Cl *HORL* RH6.....56 C3
 RDKG RH5.....40 B5
Harecroft *DORK* RH4.....40 A1
 LHD/OX KT22.....8 D3
Harendon *KWD/TDW/WH* KT20.....13 G1
Harewood Cl *REIG* RH2.....34 A2
Harkness Cl *EW* KT17.....6 C1
Haroldslea Cl *HORL* RH6.....57 G5
Haroldslea Dr *HORL* RH6.....57 G5
Harps Oak La *REDH* RH1.....15 H5
Harpswood Cl *COUL/CHIP* CR5.....16 C2
Harpurs *KWD/TDW/WH* KT20.....13 H1
Harrington Cl *REIG* RH2.....51 E1
Harriotts Cl *ASHTD* KT21.....3 H5
Harriotts La *ASHTD* KT21.....3 G4
Harrison Cl *REIG* RH2.....33 H5
Harrow Cl *DORK* RH4.....40 A2
Harrowlands Pk *DORK* RH4.....40 B2
Harrow Rd East *DORK* RH4.....40 B3
Harrow Rd West *DORK* RH4.....40 A4
Harrowsley Ct *HORL* RH6.....57 F2
Hart Cl *REDH* RH1.....37 H3
Hart Gdns *DORK* RH4.....29 F5
Hartington Cl *REIG* RH2.....33 G2
Hartington Pl *REIG* RH2 *.....33 G2
Hart Rd *DORK* RH4.....29 F5
Hartspiece Rd *REDH* RH1.....46 B1
Hartswood *RDKG* RH5.....40 D4
Hartswood Av *REIG* RH2.....44 C3
Harvestside *HORL* RH6.....57 G2
Harwood Pk *REDH* RH1.....54 A3
Hatch Gdns *KWD/TDW/WH* KT20.....6 B5
Hatchgate *HORL* RH6.....56 D4
Hatch La *REDH* RH1.....47 F5
Hatfield Rd *ASHTD* KT21.....4 B4
Hathersham La *HORL* RH6.....55 H3
Hatherwood *LHD/OX* KT22.....10 D1

Hawes Rd *KWD/TDW/WH* KT20.....6 D5
Hawk's Hl *LHD/OX* KT22.....9 H3
Hawks Hill Cl *LHD/OX* KT22.....9 H3
Hawks Hill Ct *LHD/OX* KT22.....9 H3
Hawkwood Dell *GT/LBKH* KT23.....18 C1
Hawkwood Ri *GT/LBKH* KT23.....18 C1
Hawthorn Cl *REDH* RH1.....46 A4
Hawthorn Wy *REDH* RH1.....46 B1
The Hayes *EPSOM* KT18.....5 F4
Hayfields *HORL* RH6.....57 G2
Hazel Cl *REIG* RH2.....44 D1
Hazelhurst *HORL* RH6.....57 G2
Hazelmere Cl *LHD/OX* KT22.....3 F4
Hazel Pde *LHD/OX* KT22 *.....9 E2
Hazel Rd *REIG* RH2.....45 E2
Hazel Wy *LHD/OX* KT22.....9 E2
Hazelwood Cl *LHD/OX* KT22.....9 E3
Hazelwood *DORK* RH4 *.....40 D2
Headley Common Rd
 EPSOM KT18.....22 B3
Headley Dr *EPSOM* KT18.....6 C4
Headley Gv *EPSOM* KT18.....22 B3
 KWD/TDW/WH KT20.....6 B5
Headley Heath Ap
 KWD/TDW/WH KT20.....21 H5
Headley La *RDKG* RH5.....20 C4
Headley Pde *EPSOM* KT18 *.....5 F4
Headley Rd *EPSOM* KT18.....5 E5
 LHD/OX KT22.....10 C1
Heathcote *KWD/TDW/WH* KT20.....13 H2
Heathdene *KWD/TDW/WH* KT20.....7 E4
Heath Dr *KWD/TDW/WH* KT20.....23 F1
Heather Cl *KWD/TDW/WH* KT20.....14 A2
 REDH RH1.....35 F1
Heatherlands *HORL* RH6.....57 G2
Heatherside Cl *GT/LBKH* KT23.....8 B5
Heathers Land *DORK* RH4.....40 C4
Heathfield Cl *ASHTD* KT21.....3 G4
Heathfield Dr *REDH* RH1.....45 G4
Heath Hl *DORK* RH4.....40 B1
Heathlands
 KWD/TDW/WH KT20.....13 H2
Heath Ri *DORK* RH4.....39 E3
Heathside Ct
 KWD/TDW/WH KT20.....13 F3
Heathside Pl *EPSOM* KT18.....6 D3
Hedingham Cl *HORL* RH6.....57 G2
Heights Cl *BNSTD* SM7.....7 E1
Hemlock Cl *KWD/TDW/WH* KT20.....14 A3
Henbit Cl *KWD/TDW/WH* KT20.....6 B4
Henfold La *RDKG* RH5.....49 E4
Heritage Lawn *HORL* RH6.....57 G2
Heron Ct *DORK* RH4 *.....29 E5
Heronswood Cl *HORL* RH6.....57 F2
Herons Wood Ct *HORL* RH6 *.....57 F2
Heston Rd *REDH* RH1.....45 H4
Hethersett Cl *REIG* RH2.....34 B1
Hevers Av *HORL* RH6.....56 D2
Hewers Wy *KWD/TDW/WH* KT20.....6 B5
Heymede *LHD/OX* KT22.....10 C3
Highacre *DORK* RH4.....40 B4
Highcroft Ct *GT/LBKH* KT23.....8 B5
Highfields *ASHTD* KT21.....3 H4
 LHD/OX KT22.....9 F4
Highlands Av *LHD/OX* KT22.....10 D3
Highlands Cl *LHD/OX* KT22.....10 D3
Highlands Pk *LHD/OX* KT22.....10 D3
Highlands Rd *LHD/OX* KT22.....10 D3
 REIG RH2.....34 B3
High Meadow Cl *DORK* RH4.....40 B4
High Vw *COUL/CHIP* CR5.....15 G4
High St *DORK* RH4.....40 B1
 GT/LBKH KT23.....8 D5
 HORL RH6.....57 F3
 KWD/TDW/WH KT20.....13 G3
 LHD/OX KT22.....10 B2
 REDH RH1.....26 B3
 REDH RH1.....34 D4
 REDH RH1.....38 B4
 REIG RH2.....37 F3
 REIG RH2.....33 H5
High Trees Rd *REIG* RH2.....34 B5
High View Ct *REIG* RH2 *.....34 B4
Highwoods *LHD/OX* KT22.....10 C1
Hildenley Cl *REDH* RH1.....35 E4
The Hildens *DORK* RH4.....39 E3
Hillcrest *KWD/TDW/WH* KT20 *.....30 D1
Hilley Field La *LHD/OX* KT22.....9 F2
Hillfield Cl *REDH* RH1.....35 E4
Hillfield Rd *REDH* RH1.....35 E4
Hillford Pl *REDH* RH1.....46 A5
Hill House Dr *REIG* RH2.....44 D1
Hill La *KWD/TDW/WH* KT20.....14 A1
Hill Pk *LHD/OX* KT22 *.....3 E1
Hill Park Ct *LHD/OX* KT22 *.....2 D4
Hill Park Dr *LHD/OX* KT22.....2 D4
Hill Ri *DORK* RH4.....29 E4
Hill Rd *LHD/OX* KT22.....8 D2

Hillside Cl *BNSTD* SM7.....7 E1
 BRKHM/BTCW RH3.....30 C5
Hillside Gdns
 BRKHM/BTCW RH3.....30 C4
Hillside Rd *ASHTD* KT21.....4 B2
Hilltop Cl *LHD/OX* KT22.....10 C3
Hilltop La *CTHM* CR3.....17 G5
 REDH RH1.....27 G1
Hilltop Ri *GT/LBKH* KT23.....19 E1
Hilltop Rd *REIG* RH2.....44 D1
Hill Vw *RDKG* RH5.....29 G5
Hill View Cl *KWD/TDW/WH* KT20.....13 G1
Hillview Dr *REDH* RH1.....35 E5
Hine Cl *COUL/CHIP* CR5.....16 C2
Hitchings Wy *REIG* RH2.....44 C3
Hitherwood Cl *REIG* RH2.....34 B2
Hogscross La *COUL/CHIP* CR5.....15 H2
Hogtrough La *REDH* RH1.....35 H5
Holcon Ct *REDH* RH1.....35 E1
Hole Hl *DORK* RH4.....38 D1
Holland Cl *REDH* RH1.....34 D4
Hollis Rw *REDH* RH1 *.....45 H1
Holly Hough
 KWD/TDW/WH KT20.....21 H5
Holly La East *BNSTD* SM7.....7 H1
Holly La West *BNSTD* SM7.....7 H1
Holly Lodge (Mobile Home Park)
 KWD/TDW/WH KT20.....14 A5
Holly Rd *REIG* RH2.....44 D1
Holmbury Dr *RDKG* RH5.....40 C4
Holmbury Keep *HORL* RH6.....57 G2
Holmcroft *KWD/TDW/WH* KT20.....13 F5
Holmesdale Pk *REDH* RH1 *.....36 B4
Holmesdale Rd *RDKG* RH5.....40 B5
 REDH RH1.....47 F1
 REIG RH2.....33 H3
Holmesdale Ter *RDKG* RH5 *.....40 B5
Holmethorpe Av *REDH* RH1.....35 F1
Holmwood View Rd *RDKG* RH5.....48 B2
Holsart Cl
 KWD/TDW/WH KT20.....13 F2
Home Cl *LHD/OX* KT22.....9 F1
Home Farm Cl
 BRKHM/BTCW RH3.....31 G5
 EPSOM KT18.....6 D2
Homefield Cl *HORL* RH6.....57 F2
 LHD/OX KT22.....10 C1
Homefield Gdns
 KWD/TDW/WH KT20.....6 C5
Homelands *LHD/OX* KT22.....10 C1
Home Meadow *BNSTD* SM7.....7 G1
Honeycrock La *REDH* RH1.....54 A1
Honeysuckle Cl *HORL* RH6.....57 G2
Hooley La *REDH* RH1.....34 D5
The Hoppety
 KWD/TDW/WH KT20.....13 H2
Horley Lodge La *REDH* RH1.....53 H3
Horley Rd *REDH* RH1.....45 H4
Horley Rw *HORL* RH6.....56 D2
Hornbeam Rd *REIG* RH2.....45 E2
Horsecroft *BNSTD* SM7.....7 F2
Horsecroft Mdw
 BNSTD SM7 *.....7 G1
Horsham Rd *DORK* RH4.....40 A2
 RDKG RH5.....48 C4
Howard Cl *ASHTD* KT21.....4 B4
 KWD/TDW/WH KT20.....12 D5
 LHD/OX KT22.....10 C3
Howard Pl *REIG* RH2.....33 G3
Howard Rd *DORK* RH4.....40 A1
 GT/LBKH KT23.....18 D2
 REIG RH2.....33 H5
Huddleston Crs *REDH* RH1.....26 D3
Hudsons *KWD/TDW/WH* KT20.....13 H1
Hulton Cl *LHD/OX* KT22.....10 C3
Humphrey Cl *LHD/OX* KT22.....9 E2
Huntersfield Cl *REIG* RH2.....33 H1
Hunters Ga *REDH* RH1.....36 B3
Huntingdon Rd *REDH* RH1.....34 D4
Hurst Cl *EPSOM* KT18.....12 A4
Hurst Dr *KWD/TDW/WH* KT20.....23 E1
Hurst La *EPSOM* KT18.....12 B3
Hurstleigh Cl *REDH* RH1.....34 D2
Hurstleigh Dr *REDH* RH1.....34 D2
Hurst Rd *EPSOM* KT18.....12 C3
 HORL RH6.....56 C2
Hutchins Wy *HORL* RH6.....56 D1

I

Ifield Cl *REDH* RH1.....45 G2
Ifold Rd *REDH* RH1.....46 A1
Imperial Pk *LHD/OX* KT22 *.....3 E5
Inholms La *RDKG* RH5.....40 C5
Institute Rd *DORK* RH4.....39 E2
Ironsbottom *REIG* RH2.....52 B4
Isbells Dr *REIG* RH2.....44 D1

Ivydene Cl *REDH* RH1.....46 B4

J

Jasmine Cl *REDH* RH1.....46 A
Jason Cl *REDH* RH1.....45 G
Jennings Wy *HORL* RH6.....57 H
Jennys Wy *COUL/CHIP* CR5.....16 C
Jolliffe Rd *REDH* RH1.....26 C
Jordans Cl *REDH* RH1.....46 A
Josephine Av
 KWD/TDW/WH KT20.....24 B
Josephine Cl
 KWD/TDW/WH KT20.....24 B
Jubilee Ter *BRKHM/BTCW* RH3.....42 A
 DORK RH4.....29 F
Junction Rd *DORK* RH4.....40 A
June La *REDH* RH1.....54 E
Juniper Cl *REIG* RH2.....45 E
Juniper Rd *REIG* RH2.....45 E

K

Keats Av *REDH* RH1.....35 F
Kelsey Cl *HORL* RH6.....56 F
Kelvin Av *LHD/OX* KT22.....2 E
Kendal Cl *REIG* RH2.....34 A
Kenilworth Cl *BNSTD* SM7.....7 E
Kennel Cl *HORL* RH6.....56 C
 LHD/OX KT22.....9
Kenrick Sq *REDH* RH1.....37 G
Kentwyns Ri *REDH* RH1.....56 E
Kenya Ct *HORL* RH6 *.....56
Keppel Rd *DORK* RH4.....29
Keswick Rd *GT/LBKH* KT23.....9
Kidborough Down
 GT/LBKH KT23.....18
Kidworth Cl *HORL* RH6.....56
Kilmarnock Pk *REIG* RH2.....33
Kiln La *BRKHM/BTCW* RH3.....30
 HORL RH6.....56
Kimberley Cl *HORL* RH6.....56
Kingfisher Ct *DORK* RH4 *.....29
Kingfisher Dr *REDH* RH1.....35
Kings Av *REDH* RH1.....35
Kingsbrook *LHD/OX* KT22.....9
Kings Ct *KWD/TDW/WH* KT20.....13
Kingscroft Rd *LHD/OX* KT22.....10
Kings Cross La *REDH* RH1.....47
Kingsdene *KWD/TDW/WH* KT20.....13
Kingslea *LHD/OX* KT22.....9
Kingsley Cl *HORL* RH6.....56
Kingsley Gv *REIG* RH2.....44
Kingsley Rd *HORL* RH6.....56
Kings Md *REDH* RH1.....47
Kings Mill La *REDH* RH1.....47
Kings Rd *HORL* RH6.....57
Kingston Av *LHD/OX* KT22.....10
Kingston House Gdns
 LHD/OX KT22 *.....10
Kingston Rd *LHD/OX* KT22.....10
Kingswood Rd
 KWD/TDW/WH KT20.....13
Kinnersley Mnr *REIG* RH2 *.....52
Kinnersley Wk *REIG* RH2.....6
Kipings *KWD/TDW/WH* KT20.....13
Knighton Rd *REDH* RH1.....46
Knights Pl *REDH* RH1.....46
Knightwood Cl *REIG* RH2.....44
Knoll Rd *DORK* RH4.....40
The Knolls *EW* KT17.....6
The Knoll *LHD/OX* KT22.....10
The Knowle
 KWD/TDW/WH KT20 *.....13

L

Ladbroke Gv *REDH* RH1.....46
Ladbroke Rd *HORL* RH6.....57
 REDH RH1.....46
Ladygate Cl *RDKG* RH5.....40
Ladygate Rd *RDKG* RH5.....40
Laglands Cl *REIG* RH2.....44
Lake La *HORL* RH6.....57
Lakeside *REDH* RH1.....35
Lake Vw *RDKG* RH5.....40
Lambyn Cft *HORL* RH6.....57
Landen Pk *HORL* RH6.....57
Langaller La *LHD/OX* KT22.....9
Lang Cl *LHD/OX* KT22.....9
Langley Cl *EPSOM* KT18.....5
Langley La *EPSOM* KT18.....5

Langley Vale Rd EPSOM KT18 ....5 G3
Langshott HORL 57 H2
Langshott La HORL RH6......57 G2
Langwood Cl ASHTD KT21 ....4 C2
Larch Cl KWD/TDW/WH KT20...15 E1
   REDH RH1 ......45 E1
Larchwood Cl BNSTD SM7 ......7 E1
Larksfield HORL 57 F2
Larkspur Wy RDKG RH5 ......40 D4
atimer Ct REDH RH1 ......45 H1
The Laurels BNSTD SM7 ......7 F2
avender Cl LHD/OX KT22 ......10 C2
   REDH RH1 ......46 B4
avender Cottages
   LHD/OX KT22 * 10 C2
awrence La
   BRKHM/BTCW RH3 ......32 B2
axton Gdns REDH RH1 ......26 D3
azell Gdns BRKHM/BTCW RH3....42 A5
each Gv LHD/OX KT22 ......10 C2
easide GT/LBKH KT23 ......8 C3
eatherhead By-Pass Rd
   LHD/OX KT22 ......10 C4
eatherhead Rd ASHTD KT21 ....4 A5
   GT/LBKH KT23 ......18 D1
   LHD/OX KT22 ......10 C1
eazes Av CTHM CR3 ......17 C3
echford Rd HORL RH6 ......56 D5
edbury Rd REIG RH2 ......33 G4
ee Acre DORK RH4 * 40 C4
eech La EPSOM KT18 ......22 A1
ee St HORL RH6 ......56 C2
igh Place Rd REIG RH2 ......43 E5
igh Rd BRKHM/BTCW RH3 ......42 A5
ith Vw RDKG RH5 ......40 C5
May Cl HORL RH6 ......57 E2
ret Wy LHD/OX KT22 ......10 A1
sbourne Rd REIG RH2 ......33 H5
slie Rd DORK RH4 ......29 H4
vett Rd LHD/OX KT22 ......3 F5
ey Dr KWD/TDW/WH KT20 ......14 D2
iott's La LHD/OX KT22 ......3 E4
ne La REIG RH2 ......44 D2
nes Av HORL RH6 ......57 F1
e Limes LHD/OX KT22 ......10 B3
e Tree Cl GT/LBKH KT23 ......8 C3
neway Ter DORK RH4 ......29 E4
ce La DORK RH4 ......39 F1
coln Cl HORL RH6 ......57 E4
coln Rd DORK RH4 ......29 G4
den Cl KWD/TDW/WH KT20 ......6 D5
den Ct LHD/OX KT22 ......10 C1
den Cl LHD/OX KT22 ......10 C1
den Lea DORK RH4 * 40 C4
den Pit Pth LHD/OX KT22 ......10 B1
den Rd LHD/OX KT22 ......10 B1
dens Cl EHSLY KT24 ......18 A3
kfield Cnr REDH RH1 ......34 C4
kfield Gdns REDH RH1 ......34 C4
kfield La REDH RH1 ......34 D3
kfield St REDH RH1 ......34 C4
ts Brow LHD/OX KT22 ......9 G4
s Cl ASHTD KT21 ......3 G2
s Pl ASHTD KT21 ......3 H2
s Rd ASHTD KT21 ......3 G2
s View Av
   BRKHM/BTCW RH3 ......30 C5
s Wy EHSLY KT24 ......18 A3
ell Rd REDH RH1 ......35 E5
e Bookham St
   GT/LBKH KT23 ......18 B1
e Borough
   BRKHM/BTCW RH3 ......30 C5
e Chesters
   WD/TDW/WH KT20 ......13 C5
e Collins REDH RH1 * 55 H4
Common REDH RH1 ......36 D2
e East Fld
   OUL/CHIP CR5 ......16 C1
Gv DORK RH4 * 40 C3
ton La REIG RH2 ......44 A1
e Cl LHD/OX KT22 ......9 F2
KG RH5 ......40 C5
e La RDKG RH5 ......49 F4
OH RH1 ......53 G2
e Rd LHD/OX KT22 ......9 E2
on Loop COUL/CHIP CR5...17 F1
on Rd DORK RH4 ......29 F5
on Rd South REDH RH1 ......35 E3
G RH2 ......33 G3
on Rd North REDH RH1 ......26 C1
on Rd South REDH RH1 ......26 B5
tome La REIG RH2 ......53 F1
ridge Rd HORL RH6 ......56 D5
bridge Wk HORL RH6 ......56 D5
bridge Wy HORL RH6 ......56 D5
champ Cl HORL RH6 ......57 G3
Copse GT/LBKH KT23 ......8 D3

Longfield Crs
   KWD/TDW/WH KT20 ......6 C5
Longfield Rd DORK RH4 ......39 H2
Longheath Dr GT/LBKH KT23 ......8 A4
Longmeadow GT/LBKH KT23 ......8 B5
Longmere Gdns
   KWD/TDW/WH KT20 ......6 C4
Long Shaw LHD/OX KT22 ......3 E4
Long Wk EPSOM KT18 ......5 E2
Lonsdale Rd DORK RH4 ......29 F5
Loop Rd EPSOM KT18 ......5 E2
Loraine Gdns ASHTD KT21 ......4 A2
Lordsgrove Cl
   KWD/TDW/WH KT20 ......6 B5
Lorian Dr REIG RH2 ......34 A3
The Lorne GT/LBKH KT23 ......18 C1
Lothian Wd
   KWD/TDW/WH KT20 ......13 F2
Lovelands La
   KWD/TDW/WH KT20 ......24 D2
Love La KWD/TDW/WH KT20 ......22 D2
Lowburys DORK RH4 ......40 A4
Lower Bridge Rd REDH RH1......34 D4
Lower Rd GT/LBKH KT23 ......18 B1
   LHD/OX KT22 ......9 G3
   REDH RH1 ......45 F1
Lower Shott GT/LBKH KT23 ......18 C1
Lumley Rd HORL RH6 ......57 E3
Lusteds Cl REDH RH1 ......40 C4
The Lye KWD/TDW/WH KT20 ......13 G2
Lymden Gdns REIG RH2 ......44 D1
Lyme Regis Rd BNSTD SM7 ......7 F2
Lyndale Rd REDH RH1 ......35 C2
Lyndhurst Rd REIG RH2 ......44 D1
Lynn Wk REIG RH2 ......44 D3
Lynwood Rd REDH RH1 ......35 E2
Lyons Ct DORK RH4 ......40 B1
Lyonsdene
   KWD/TDW/WH KT20 ......24 B2
Lywood Cl KWD/TDW/WH KT20...13 G2

M

Mabbotts KWD/TDW/WH KT20...13 H1
Maddox La GT/LBKH KT23 ......8 B4
Maddox Pk GT/LBKH KT23 ......8 A3
Madeira Wk REIG RH2 ......34 B3
Magazine Pl LHD/OX KT22 ......10 C2
Magazine Rd CTHM CR3 ......17 H2
Magnolia Ct HORL RH6 * 57 E3
Magnolia Wy RDKG RH5 ......40 D4
Maizecroft HORL RH6 ......57 G2
Malcolm Gdns HORL RH6 ......56 B5
Mallard Cl KWD/TDW/WH KT20...6 B4
   REDH RH1 ......35 E1
Mallard Ct DORK RH4 * 29 E5
Malmstone Av REDH RH1 ......26 C3
Mannamead EPSOM KT18 ......5 G4
Mannamead Cl EPSOM KT18......5 G4
Manor Cl HORL RH6 ......56 D3
Manor Dr HORL RH6 ......56 D3
Manorhouse La GT/LBKH KT23...18 A1
Manor La KWD/TDW/WH KT20......24 C4
Manor Pl GT/LBKH KT23 ......18 C1
Manor Rd REDH RH1 ......26 C4
   REIG RH2 ......33 F2
Manor Wy LHD/OX KT22 ......2 A1
Mansfield Dr REDH RH1 ......26 D3
Maplehurst LHD/OX KT22 ......9 F3
Maple Rd ASHTD KT21 ......3 H4
   REDH RH1 ......45 H4
Maple Wy COUL/CHIP CR5 ......16 B1
Marbles Wy KWD/TDW/WH KT20...6 D4
Margery Gv
   KWD/TDW/WH KT20 ......24 A4
Margery La
   KWD/TDW/WH KT20 ......24 B4
Markedge La COUL/CHIP CR5...15 H4
   REDH RH1 ......25 H2
Market Field Rd REDH RH1 ......34 D3
Marketfield Wy REDH RH1 ......34 D4
Mark Oak La LHD/OX KT22 ......8 A5
Mark St REIG RH2 ......33 H3
Marlborough Hl DORK RH4 ......40 B1
The Marld ASHTD KT21 ......4 A3
Marley Ri DORK RH4 ......40 A4
Martineau Dr DORK RH4 ......40 B3
Mason's Bridge Rd REDH RH1...46 C5
Masons Paddock DORK RH4......29 E4
Massetts Rd HORL RH6 ......56 D4
Matthew's St REIG RH2 ......33 H3
Maybury Cl KWD/TDW/WH KT20...7 E4
Mayell Cl LHD/OX KT22 ......10 C3
Mayfield LHD/OX KT22 ......10 C3
Mayfield Rd REDH RH1 ......46 A5
Mayfield Gn GT/LBKH KT23 ......18 C2

Mead Av REDH RH1 ......54 A2
Mead Cl REDH RH1 ......35 E1
Mead Crs GT/LBKH KT23 ......8 C5
Mead End ASHTD KT21 ......4 A3
Meadowbrook Rd DORK RH4...29 E5
Meadow La LHD/OX KT22 ......9 E2
Meadow Rd ASHTD KT21 ......4 A2
Meadowside GT/LBKH KT23 ......8 C3
   HORL RH6 ......57 F2
Meadow Wk
   KWD/TDW/WH KT20 ......13 F4
Meadow Wy GT/LBKH KT23 ......8 D3
   KWD/TDW/WH KT20 ......7 E2
   REIG RH2 ......44 D3
The Mead ASHTD KT21 ......4 A4
   DORK RH4 * 40 C4
Meadway EHSLY KT24 ......18 A3
The Meadway HORL RH6 ......57 G3
Meare Cl KWD/TDW/WH KT20......13 G5
Meath Green Av HORL RH6 ......56 D2
Meath Green La HORL RH6 ......53 C5
Mede Fld LHD/OX KT22 ......9 F4
Melton Rd REDH RH1 ......26 C5
Melvinshaw LHD/OX KT22 ......10 C1
Meon Cl KWD/TDW/WH KT20......13 F2
Merefield Gdns
   KWD/TDW/WH KT20 ......6 D4
Mere Rd KWD/TDW/WH KT20......13 F4
Meridian Gv HORL RH6 ......57 G2
Merland Cl KWD/TDW/WH KT20...6 C5
Merland Gn KWD/TDW/WH KT20...6 C5
Merland Ri KWD/TDW/WH KT20...6 C4
Merrylands Farm GT/LBKH KT23...8 A4
Merrylands Rd GT/LBKH KT23......8 B3
Merrywood Gv
   KWD/TDW/WH KT20 ......23 H5
Merrywood Pk REIG RH2 ......33 H2
Merstham Rd REDH RH1 ......27 G5
Merton Gdns
   KWD/TDW/WH KT20 ......6 D4
Merton Wy LHD/OX KT22 ......3 F4
The Mews REIG RH2 * 33 F3
Michael Crs HORL RH6 ......57 E5
Michelham Gdns
   KWD/TDW/WH KT20 * 6 C5
Mickleham Dr LHD/OX KT22 ......20 C1
Middlefield HORL RH6 ......57 G2
Middlemead Cl GT/LBKH KT23...8 C5
Middlemead Rd GT/LBKH KT23...8 B5
Middle Rd LHD/OX KT22 ......10 B1
Middle St BRKHM/BTCW RH3......41 H1
Mid Holmwood La RDKG RH5...48 C2
Mid St REDH RH1 ......47 F1
Miena Wy ASHTD KT21 ......3 H2
Milford Ct RDKG RH5 ......48 C5
Millbottom La RDKG RH5 ......48 D4
Mill Cl GT/LBKH KT23 ......8 C4
   HORL RH6 ......56 C2
Millers Copse EPSOM KT18 ......5 F4
   REDH RH1 ......55 H4
Miller's La REDH RH1 ......55 H4
Millfield La KWD/TDW/WH KT20...14 C5
Mill Hl BRKHM/BTCW RH3 ......30 D5
Mill Hill La BRKHM/BTCW RH3...30 D4
Mill La DORK RH4 ......29 F5
   HORL RH6 ......56 B3
   KWD/TDW/WH KT20 ......13 H3
   LHD/OX KT22 ......10 A2
   REDH RH1 ......35 G1
Mill Rd KWD/TDW/WH KT20......13 H3
   RDKG RH5 ......48 C4
Millside Ct GT/LBKH KT23 * 8 C5
Millstead Cl
   KWD/TDW/WH KT20 ......13 F3
Mill St REDH RH1 ......34 C5
Millview Cl REIG RH2 ......34 B2
Mill Wy LHD/OX KT22 ......11 F5
Millway REIG RH2 ......34 B4
Milton Av DORK RH4 ......39 F2
Miltoncourt La DORK RH4 ......39 G1
Milton St DORK RH4 ......39 F2
Milton Wy LHD/OX KT22 ......9 E5
Minchin Cl LHD/OX KT22 ......10 A2
Mint Gdns DORK RH4 ......29 E5
Mint La KWD/TDW/WH KT20......24 C4
Mistley Gdns HORL RH6 ......56 B4
Moat Ct ASHTD KT21 ......4 A2
Moats La REDH RH1 ......47 F5
Mogador Rd
   KWD/TDW/WH KT20 ......24 A3
Mole Rd LHD/OX KT22 ......9 F1
Mole Valley Pl ASHTD KT21 ......3 H4
Monks Cl LHD/OX KT22 ......9 E1
Monks Rd BNSTD SM7 ......7 G2
Monk's Wk REIG RH2 ......33 H4
Monkswell La COUL/CHIP CR5...14 D4
Monson Rd REDH RH1 ......34 D1
Montfort Ri REDH RH1 ......53 H2
Montrouge Crs EW KT17 ......6 C1

Moore's Rd DORK RH4 ......29 F5
Moorfield RDKG RH5 * 48 D4
The Moorings GT/LBKH KT23 ......8 C5
Moor Pk HORL RH6 * 57 F4
Morden Cl KWD/TDW/WH KT20...6 D5
Morris Rd REDH RH1 ......47 E1
Morston Cl KWD/TDW/WH KT20...6 B5
Morton KWD/TDW/WH KT20 ......13 H1
Mosford Cl HORL RH6 ......56 D1
Mostyn Ter REDH RH1 ......35 E5
Motts Hill La
   KWD/TDW/WH KT20 ......13 F2
Mount Cl LHD/OX KT22 ......9 H3
The Mount Dr REIG RH2 ......34 A2
Mount Pleasant EHSLY KT24...18 A3
Mount Ri REDH RH1 ......45 F1
Mount St DORK RH4 ......29 E5
The Mount KWD/TDW/WH KT20...24 B1
   LHD/OX KT22 ......9 G1
Mountview Cl REDH RH1 ......45 G1
Mountview Dr REDH RH1 ......45 G1
Mowbray Gdns DORK RH4......29 F4
Mulberry Ga BNSTD SM7 ......7 F1
Murrells Wk GT/LBKH KT23 ......8 C3
The Murreys ASHTD KT21 ......3 H3
Myrtle Cottages DORK RH4 * 40 B4
Myrtle Rd DORK RH4 ......29 E5

N

Nailsworth Crs REDH RH1 ......26 D4
Nash Gdns REDH RH1 ......34 D2
Netherleigh Pk REDH RH1......47 E2
Netherne Dr COUL/CHIP CR5...16 C2
Netherne La COUL/CHIP CR5...16 C2
New Battlebridge La REDH RH1...26 B5
New Cswy REIG RH2 ......44 D2
New Cottages DORK RH4 * 39 H2
   REIG RH2 ......32 D2
Newenham Rd GT/LBKH KT23...18 C1
New House La REDH RH1 ......54 D1
Newlands Cl HORL RH6 ......56 D1
New North Rd REIG RH2 ......44 B2
New Pde DORK RH4 * 29 F5
   GT/LBKH KT23 * 19 E1
New Place Gdns REDH RH1......34 D3
New Rd KWD/TDW/WH KT20...24 C2
Newstead Hall HORL RH6 ......57 H4
Newton Wood Rd ASHTD KT21...4 C1
Nightingale Wy REDH RH1 ......37 G4
Ninth Av KWD/TDW/WH KT20 *...24 B1
Noke Dr REDH RH1 ......35 E3
Norbury Rd REIG RH2 ......33 F4
Norbury Wy GT/LBKH KT23 ......9 E5
Norfolk Cl HORL RH6 ......57 E4
Norfolk La RDKG RH5 ......48 B2
Norfolk Rd DORK RH4 ......40 A1
   RDKG RH5 ......48 C5
Nork Ri BNSTD SM7 ......6 D1
Norman Cl EPSOM KT18 ......6 B4
North Cl RDKG RH5 ......40 C5
North Downs Wy
   BRKHM/BTCW RH3 ......22 D5
   CTHM CR3 ......27 H1
   KWD/TDW/WH KT20 ......30 B2
   RDKG RH5 ......28 C3
   REIG RH2 ......24 D5
Northfields ASHTD KT21 ......4 A4
Northgate Rd HORL RH6 ......56 D5
North Md REDH RH1 ......34 D1
North Rd REIG RH2 ......44 B2
North Station Ap REDH RH1 *...47 F1
North St DORK RH4 ......40 A1
   LHD/OX KT22 ......10 A2
   REDH RH1 ......34 D3
North View Crs EPSOM KT18......5 F4
Norwood Cl EHSLY KT24 ......18 A3
Norwood Rd EHSLY KT24 ......18 A3
Nower Rd DORK RH4 ......40 A1
Nursery Cl
   KWD/TDW/WH KT20 ......13 F5
Nursery La HORL RH6 ......56 B4
Nursery Rd
   KWD/TDW/WH KT20 ......13 F5
Nutcombe La DORK RH4 ......39 H1
Nutcroft Gv LHD/OX KT22......9 G2
Nutfield Marsh Rd REDH RH1...35 H1
Nutfield Pk REDH RH1 ......47 G3
Nutfield Rd REDH RH1 ......35 F4
Nuthatch Gdns REIG RH2 ......45 E3
Nutley La REIG RH2 ......33 F3
Nutwood Av
   BRKHM/BTCW RH3 ......31 E5
Nutwood Cl BRKHM/BTCW RH3...31 E5
Nyefield Pk
   KWD/TDW/WH KT20 ......23 E1

O

Oakbank *LHD/OX* KT22 ....9 E3
Oak Cl *KWD/TDW/WH* KT20 ....21 H5
Oakdene *KWD/TDW/WH* KT20 ......7 E5
Oakdene Cl *BRKHM/BTCW* RH3....42 A1
GT/LBKH KT23 ....19 E2
Oakdene Rd *BRKHM/BTCW* RH3...41 H1
GT/LBKH KT23 ....8 B4
REDH RH1 ....34 D4
Oak Dr *KWD/TDW/WH* KT20 ....31 E1
Oaken Coppice *ASHTD* KT21 ....4 C4
Oakfield Dr *REIG* RH2 ....33 C2
Oakfield Rd *ASHTD* KT21 ....4 A3
Oak Hl *LHD/OX* KT18 ....5 F1
Oakhill Cl *ASHTD* KT21 ....3 C3
Oakhill Rd *ASHTD* KT21 ....3 C3
REIG RH2 ....33 H5
Oaklands *HORL* RH6 ....57 C3
LHD/OX KT22 ....9 F4
Oaklands Dr *REDH* RH1 ....46 B1
Oaklands Wy
KWD/TDW/WH KT20 ....13 G2
Oaklawn Rd *LHD/OX* KT22 ....2 C3
Oakley Gdns *BRKHM/BTCW* RH3..42 A5
Oak Lodge Dr *REDH* RH1 ....54 A2
Oak Rdg *DORK* RH4....................40 B4
Oak Rd *LHD/OX* KT22 ....3 E4
REIG RH2 ....33 H3
Oaks Cl *LHD/OX* KT22 ....10 A1
Oakside Ct *HORL* RH6 ....57 G2
Oakside La *HORL* RH6 ....57 G2
Oaks La *RDKG* RH5 ....48 B2
Oaks Rd *REIG* RH2 ....34 B3
The Oaks *DORK* RH4 * 40 B4
Oaks Wy *EPSOM* KT18 ....6 A4
Oak Wy *ASHTD* KT21 ....4 C1
REIG RH2 ....34 B5
Oakwood Cl *REDH* RH1 ....35 E4
REDH RH1 * 47 F1
Oakwood Rd *HORL* RH6 ....57 G2
REDH RH1 ....27 G4
Oatfield Rd
KWD/TDW/WH KT20 ....13 F1
Oatlands *HORL* RH6 ....57 F2
Oatlands Rd *KWD/TDW/WH* KT20..7 E4
Old Barn Rd *EPSOM* KT18 ....5 E2
Old Char Whf *DORK* RH4.............28 D5
Old Ct *ASHTD* KT21 ....4 A4
Oldfield Gdns *ASHTD* KT21 ....3 H4
Oldfield Rd *HORL* RH6.................56 D5
Old Fox Cl *CTHM* CR3 ....17 H1
Old Kiln La *BRKHM/BTCW* RH3....31 E4
Old London Rd *EPSOM* KT18 ....6 A3
RDKG RH5 ....20 C3
Old Mill La *REDH* RH1 ....26 B3
Old Pottery Cl *REIG* RH2 ....44 D1
Old Rectory Cl
KWD/TDW/WH KT20 ....13 E4
Old Redstone Dr *REDH* RH1 ....35 E5
Old Reigate Rd
BRKHM/BTCW RH3.....................31 E4
DORK RH4.................................30 A4
Old Rd *BRKHM/BTCW* RH3..........31 H3
Old School La
BRKHM/BTCW RH3.....................41 H1
Old Station Ap *LHD/OX* KT22......10 A1
The Old Yd *REDH* RH1 ....37 E3
Orchard Cl *HORL* RH6 ....56 D2
LHD/OX KT22 ....2 D4
LHD/OX KT22 ....9 F2
Orchard Dr *ASHTD* KT21 ....3 H5
Orchard End *LHD/OX* KT22 ....9 E4
Orchard Gdns *EHSLY* KT24 ....18 A3
Orchardleigh *LHD/OX* KT22 ....10 B2
Orchard Rd *DORK* RH4 ....40 B2
REIG RH2 ....33 H4
The Orchard *HORL* RH6 * 57 E3
RDKG RH5 ....40 C5
Orchard Wy *DORK* RH4 ....40 B2
KWD/TDW/WH KT20 ....24 A1
REIG RH2 ....44 D3
Ormside Wy *REDH* RH1 ....35 F1
Orpin Rd *REDH* RH1 ....26 C5
Orwell Gdns *REIG* RH2 ....44 D1
Osborne Rd *REDH* RH1...............35 E1
Oswald Cl *LHD/OX* KT22 ....9 E2
Oswald Rd *LHD/OX* KT22 ....9 E2
Otter Meadow *LHD/OX* KT22.......2 D4
Ottways Av *ASHTD* KT21 ....3 H4
Ottways La *ASHTD* KT21 ....3 H5
Outwood La
KWD/TDW/WH KT20 ....14 D2
REDH RH1 ....37 H4
Overdale *ASHTD* KT21 ....4 A1
RDKG RH5 ....29 G5
REDH RH1 ....37 E3

Overlord Ct *LHD/OX* KT22 ....9 F1
Oveton Wy *GT/LBKH* KT23 ....18 C1
Owen Pl *LHD/OX* KT22 * 10 B2
Oxford Rd *REDH* RH1 ....34 C3
Oxshott Rd *LHD/OX* KT22 ....2 D1

P

The Paddocks *GT/LBKH* KT23........18 D1
Paddocks Wy *ASHTD* KT21...........4 A3
The Paddock *DORK* RH4 ....38 D2
Palmer Cl *HORL* RH6 ....56 D1
REDH RH1 ....35 E5
Palmerston Cl *REDH* RH1............45 G2
Paper Ms *DORK* RH4 ....29 F5
The Parade
KWD/TDW/WH KT20 * 7 E4
LHD/OX KT22 * 3 F5
Park Av *REDH* RH1 ....53 H2
Park Cl *BRKHM/BTCW* RH3.........41 H4
LHD/OX KT22 ....9 H4
Park Copse *RDKG* RH5................40 D1
Parker's Cl *ASHTD* KT21 ....4 A4
Parker's Hl *ASHTD* KT21 ....4 A4
Parker's La *ASHTD* KT21 ....4 B4
Parkgate Rd *REIG* RH2 ....33 H5
Park Gn *GT/LBKH* KT23 ....8 C4
Park Hall Rd *REIG* RH2...............33 C2
Park House Dr *REIG* RH2............44 B1
Parkhurst Gv *HORL* RH6.............56 C2
Parkhurst Rd *HORL* RH6.............56 C2
Parklands *GT/LBKH* KT23 ....8 C3
RDKG RH5 ....40 B5
Park La *ASHTD* KT21 ....4 B3
COUL/CHIP CR5...........................16 D1
REIG RH2 ....33 F5
Park La East *REIG* RH2 ....44 C1
Parklawn Av *HORL* RH6..............56 D1
Parkpale La *BRKHM/BTCW* RH3...41 G4
Park Ri *LHD/OX* KT22..................10 A1
Park Rise Rd *LHD/OX* KT22.........10 B1
Park Rd *ASHTD* KT21 ....4 A3
REDH RH1 ....34 D2
The Park *GT/LBKH* KT23 ....8 C5
Park Vw *GT/LBKH* KT23 ....8 C5
HORL RH6 ....57 E3
Park View Rd *REDH* RH1.............54 A1
Parkway *DORK* RH4....................29 E5
Park Wy *GT/LBKH* KT23 ....8 C3
Parkwood Rd *REDH* RH1 ....36 A3
Park Wood Vw *BNSTD* SM7.........6 A1
Park Works Rd *REDH* RH1...........36 B3
Parr Cl *LHD/OX* KT22....................2 D5
Parris Cft *DORK* RH4 ....40 C4
Parsonage La *DORK* RH4.............39 E2
Parsonage Sq *DORK* RH4 ....29 E5
Parsons Cl *HORL* RH6 ....56 C2
Parsonsfield Rd *BNSTD* SM7 ....6 D1
Parthia Cl *KWD/TDW/WH* KT20....6 B4
Paul's Pl *ASHTD* KT21 ....4 D4
The Pavement *REDH* RH1 * 34 D4
Pear Tree Hl *REDH* RH1 * 54 A3
Pebble Cl *EPSOM* KT18 ....22 C3
Pebblehill Rd
BRKHM/BTCW RH3.....................22 C5
Pebble La *LHD/OX* KT22 ....11 G2
Pelham Wy *GT/LBKH* KT23 ....18 D1
Pembroke Cl *BNSTD* SM7.............7 H2
Pendell Ms *REDH* RH1 * 34 D5
Pendell Rd *REDH* RH1 ....36 D1
Pendleton Cl *REDH* RH1 ....45 H1
Pendleton Rd *REDH* RH1 ....45 F2
Penrith Cl *REIG* RH2 ....34 C3
Penrose Rd *LHD/OX* KT22 ....9 E2
Pepys Cl *ASHTD* KT21 ....4 D3
Perimeter Rd North *HORL* RH6 ..56 D5
Petersmead Cl
KWD/TDW/WH KT20 ....13 G3
Petridge Rd *REDH* RH1 ....45 H4
Petters Rd *ASHTD* KT21 ....4 B1
Philanthropic Rd *REDH* RH1.......35 F5
Picketts La *REDH* RH1 ....54 C1
Picquets Wy *BNSTD* SM7 ....7 F2
Pigeonhouse La
COUL/CHIP CR5...........................15 E5
Pilgrims Cl *RDKG* RH5 ....29 G2
Pilgrims' La *CTHM* CR3...............27 F1
Pilgrims Pl *REIG* RH2..................33 G2
Pilgrims Wy *RDKG* RH5 ....29 F1
REIG RH2 ....33 G2
Pine Dean *GT/LBKH* KT23 ....8 D5
Pine Gdns *HORL* RH6 ....57 E4
Pine Hl *EPSOM* KT18 ....5 F1
Pinehurst Cl
KWD/TDW/WH KT20 ....14 C2
Pine Wk *GT/LBKH* KT23 ....8 D5
Pippbrook Gdns *DORK* RH4........29 F5

Pit Wood Gn
KWD/TDW/WH KT20......................6 C5
Pixham La *DORK* RH4 ....29 H4
Pixholme Gv *DORK* RH4..............29 G4
Place Farm Rd *REDH* RH1...........37 H1
Pleasure Pit Rd *ASHTD* KT21 ......4 D3
Pointers Hl *DORK* RH4................39 E3
The Pointers *ASHTD* KT21............4 A5
Polesden Rd *RDKG* RH5 ....18 D4
Polesden Vw *GT/LBKH* KT23 ......18 D2
Pond Farm Cl
KWD/TDW/WH KT20 ....13 F4
Poplar Av *LHD/OX* KT22 ....10 C2
Poplar Rd *LHD/OX* KT22 ....10 B2
Portland Dr *REDH* RH1 ....26 D4
Portland Rd *DORK* RH4 ....29 E5
Post House La *GT/LBKH* KT23.......8 C5
Potters Wy *REIG* RH2 ....45 E3
Pound Ct *ASHTD* KT21 ....4 B3
Pound Crs *LHD/OX* KT22 ....9 F1
Pound Rd *BNSTD* SM7 ....7 G2
Povey Cross Rd *HORL* RH6 ....56 C5
Powell Cl *HORL* RH6...................56 C2
Powells Cl *DORK* RH4 ....40 C4
Poynes Rd *HORL* RH6 ....56 C1
Premier Pde *HORL* RH6 * 57 F3
Preston Gv *ASHTD* KT21 ....3 G2
Preston La *KWD/TDW/WH* KT20...6 C5
Pretty La *COUL/CHIP* CR5 ....16 C1
Prices La *REIG* RH2 ....44 C2
Priestlands Cl *HORL* RH6............56 D2
Primrose Av *HORL* RH6..............57 F5
Prince Albert Sq *REDH* RH1........45 H4
Prince of Wales Rd *REDH* RH1....55 C2
Princes Rd *REDH* RH1 ....45 H1
Princess Wy *REDH* RH1 ....35 E3
Priors Md *GT/LBKH* KT23 ....9 E5
The Priors *ASHTD* KT21 ....3 H4
Priory Cl *DORK* RH4 ....40 A3
HORL RH6 ....56 D2
Priory Ct *DORK* RH4 * 40 B3
Priory Dr *REIG* RH2 ....44 C1
Priory Rd *REIG* RH2 ....44 C1
Proctor Gdns *GT/LBKH* KT23........8 D5
Prossers *REDH* RH1 *.................13 H1
Punchbowl La *RDKG* RH5 ....29 H5
Purbeck Cl *REDH* RH1 ....26 D4

Q

Quality St *REDH* RH1 ....26 B3
Quarry Gdns *LHD/OX* KT22 ....10 D1
Quarry Hill Pk *REIG* RH2 ....34 A1
The Quarry *BRKHM/BTCW* RH3...31 F2
Queen Annes Ct
LHD/OX KT22 ....10 B1
Queen Anne's Gdns
LHD/OX KT22 ....10 B1
Queen Annes Ms
LHD/OX KT22 ....10 B1
Queen Anne's Ter
LHD/OX KT22 ....10 B1
Queens Cl *KWD/TDW/WH* KT20..13 E4
Queens Crs *DORK* RH4 ....40 A2
Queens Rd *HORL* RH6 ....57 E3
Queensway *REDH* RH1 ....34 D3
Quennell Cl *ASHTD* KT21 ....4 B4

R

Radnor Ct *REDH* RH1..................34 C4
Radolphs *KWD/TDW/WH* KT20....13 H2
Radstock Wy *REDH* RH1 ....26 D3
Raglan Cl *REIG* RH2....................34 A2
Raglan Rd *REIG* RH2...................33 H2
Ralliwood Rd *ASHTD* KT21 ....4 C4
Ralphs Cross *GT/LBKH* KT23 * 19 E1
Ramsey Cl *HORL* RH6 ....56 D3
Randal Crs *REIG* RH2 ....44 C1
Randalls Crs *LHD/OX* KT22 ....3 E5
Randalls Park Av *LHD/OX* KT22....3 E5
Randalls Park Dr *LHD/OX* KT22...10 A1
Randalls Rd *LHD/OX* KT22 ....2 C5
Randalls Wy *LHD/OX* KT22 ....10 A1
Ranelagh Rd *REDH* RH1 ....34 C4
Ranmore Cl *REDH* RH1...............35 E1
Ranmore Common Rd
RDKG RH5 ....28 C2
Ranmore Rd *DORK* RH4 ....28 C4
Rathgar Cl *REDH* RH1 ....46 A4
Ravens Cl *REDH* RH1 ....34 D3
Raymead Cl *LHD/OX* KT22 ....9 G2
Raymead Wy *LHD/OX* KT22..........9 G2
Raymer Wk *HORL* RH6 ....57 G2

Reading Arch Rd *REDH* RH1........34 D4
Read Rd *ASHTD* KT21 ....3 H2
Reads Rest La
KWD/TDW/WH KT20......................7 G5
Rectory Cl *ASHTD* KT21 ....4 B4
Rectory La *ASHTD* KT21 ....4 B4
BRKHM/BTCW RH3.....................31 H2
GT/LBKH KT23 ....18 B1
Rectory Rd *COUL/CHIP* CR5........15 F5
Redcote Pl *DORK* RH4 ....29 H4
Redlands *RDKG* RH5 ....48 B5
Redlands La *RDKG* RH5 ....48 D3
Red La *RDKG* RH5 ....49 G1
Redleaf Cl *LHD/OX* KT22 ....9 F5
Redstone Hl *REDH* RH1 ....35 E4
Redstone Hollow *REDH* RH1.......35 E5
Redstone Mnr *REDH* RH1 ....35 E4
Redstone Pk *REDH* RH1 ....35 E4
Redstone Rd *REDH* RH1..............35 E5
Redwood Mt *REIG* RH2 ....33 G2
Reed Dr *REDH* RH1 ....46 A4
Reeve Rd *REIG* RH2 ....45 E3
Regent Cl *REDH* RH1 ....26 C1
Regent Crs *REDH* RH1 ....34 C2
Regent Pk *LHD/OX* KT22 * 3 F5
Regents Ms *HORL* RH6 ....57 E3
Reigate Hl *REIG* RH2 ....33 H1
Reigate Hill Cl *REIG* RH2............33 H1
Reigate Rd *DORK* RH4................30 A2
HORL RH6 ....56 C1
KWD/TDW/WH KT20......................6 C2
LHD/OX KT22 ....10 C4
REDH RH1 ....45 H3
REIG RH2 ....34 D2
REIG RH2 ....53 E1
The Renmans *ASHTD* KT21 ....4 D3
Rennie Ter *REDH* RH1 ....35 E4
Revell Cl *LHD/OX* KT22 ....8 D2
Revell Dr *LHD/OX* KT22 ....8 D2
Richbell Cl *ASHTD* KT21 ....3 H4
Richmond Cl *LHD/OX* KT22 ....9 F2
Richmond Wy *GT/LBKH* KT23 ....8 D5
Rickwood *HORL* RH6 ....57 F3
Ridge Cl *BRKHM/BTCW* RH3 ......41 H5
Ridgegate Cl *REIG* RH2...............34 D2
Ridge Gn *REDH* RH1 ....47 E2
Ridge Green Cl *REDH* RH1 ....47 E2
Ridgelands *LHD/OX* KT22 ....9 E4
Ridgemount Wy *REDH* RH1.........45 H4
The Ridge *EPSOM* KT18 ....5 F1
LHD/OX KT22 ....9 E4
Ridgeway Cl *DORK* RH4..............40 A2
Ridgeway Ct *REDH* RH1 * 34 C3
Ridgeway Dr *DORK* RH4.............40 A2
Ridgeway Rd *DORK* RH4 ....40 A2
REDH RH1 ....34 C3
The Ridgeway *HORL* RH6 ....57 E3
LHD/OX KT22 ....9 E4
The Ridings *ASHTD* KT21 ....3 H5
KWD/TDW/WH KT20 ....14 D2
REIG RH2 ....34 D2
Ringley Av *HORL* RH6 ....57 E3
Ringley Park Av *REIG* RH2..........34 D2
Ringley Park Rd *REIG* RH2 ....34 C2
Ringwood Av *REDH* RH1.............34 C3
The Rise *KWD/TDW/WH* KT20.....13 H1
Riverbank *DORK* RH4 * 29 H4
River Island Cl *LHD/OX* KT22.......2 D3
River La *LHD/OX* KT22 ....2 D3
Riverside *DORK* RH4 * 29 G4
HORL RH6 ....57 E4
Robin Gdns *REDH* RH1 ....34 C2
Rockshaw Rd *REDH* RH1 ....26 B1
Rocky La *REDH* RH1....................26 C2
Roebuck Cl *ASHTD* KT21 ....4 A1
REIG RH2 ....33 G4
Roffey Cl *HORL* RH6 ....56 D2
Roman Wy *LHD/OX* KT22 ....9 F2
Ronson Wy *LHD/OX* KT22.............3 E5
Rookery Cl *LHD/OX* KT22 ....9 F2
Rookery Dr *DORK* RH4 ....28 C4
Rookery Hl *ASHTD* KT21 ....4 D3
Rookery Md *COUL/CHIP* CR5.......15 G1
Rookery Wy
KWD/TDW/WH KT20 ....14 C2
Rook La *CTHM* CR3 ....17 H1
Rookwood Cl *REDH* RH1.............35 F1
Roothill La *BRKHM/BTCW* RH3...41 F5
Rosebank Cottages *REIG* RH2 * ..33 H2
Rosebery Rd *EPSOM* KT18 ....5 F1
Rose Bushes *EW* KT17..................6 A1
Rosedale *ASHTD* KT21 ....3 H4
Rose Hl *DORK* RH4 ....29 E5
Rose Hill Arch Ms *DORK* RH4 * ..29 E5
Rosemary Ct *HORL* RH6 * 57 E3
Rosemary La *HORL* RH6 ....57 E3
Rosemead Cl *REDH* RH1 ....45 G3
Roses Cottages *DORK* RH4 * 29 E5

Rothervale *HORL* RH6 ....56 D1
Rothes Rd *DORK* RH4 ....29 F5
Rough Rew *DORK* RH4 ....40 B4
Rowan Cl *REIG* RH2 ....45 E1
Rowan Gv *COUL/CHIP* CR5 ....16 B1
Rowan Md *KWD/TDW/WH* KT20 ....6 B4
Royal Dr *EPSOM* KT18 ....6 B3
Royal Earlswood Pk *REDH* RH1 ....46 A3
Ruffetts Wy
  KWD/TDW/WH KT20 ....7 E2
Rural Wy *REDH* RH1 ....35 E4
Rushett Dr *DORK* RH4 ....40 B4
Rushetts Rd *REIG* RH2 ....45 E3
Rushworth Rd *REIG* RH2 ....33 G3
Russell Cl *KWD/TDW/WH* KT20 ....13 G5
Russell Ct *LHD/OX* KT22 ....10 B2
Russells *KWD/TDW/WH* KT20 ....13 H2
Russells Crs *REIG* RH6 ....57 E4
Russet Cl *HORL* RH6 ....57 G3
Russet Wy *RDKG* RH5 ....40 D5
Rutherwick Cl *HORL* RH6 ....56 D1
Rutland Cl *ASHTD* KT21 ....4 A2
  REDH 34 D3
Rye Brook Rd *LHD/OX* KT22 ....3 E3
Rye Fld *ASHTD* KT21 ....3 H1
Ryelands *HORL* RH6 ....57 G2
Ryelands Ct *LHD/OX* KT22 ....3 E3
Rykens La *BRKHM/BTCW* RH3 ....42 A4

S

Saddlers Wy *EPSOM* KT18 ....5 F4
St Alban's Rd *REIG* RH2 ....33 G3
St Andrews *HORL* RH6 * 57 F4
St Andrew's Cl *REIG* RH2 ....33 H5
St Anne's Dr *REDH* RH1 ....35 E2
St Annes Dr North *REDH* RH1 ....35 E2
St Annes Mt *REDH* RH1 ....35 E3
St Annes Ri *REDH* RH1 ....35 E3
St Annes Wy *REDH* RH1 * 35 E3
St Aubyns *REDH* RH1 ....40 B3
St Brelades Cl *DORK* RH4 ....40 A3
St Catherine's Cross *REDH* RH1 ....37 G4
St Clair Cl *REIG* RH2 ....34 A4
St David's Cl *REIG* RH2 ....34 A3
St Georges *HORL* RH6 * 57 F4
St Georges Cl *HORL* RH6 ....57 F3
St George's Rd *REDH* RH1 ....54 D2
St Hilda's Cl *HORL* RH6 ....57 F3
St John's *RDKG* RH5 ....40 C5
St John's Av *LHD/OX* KT22 ....10 C1
St Johns Church Rd *RDKG* RH5 ....38 B4
St John's Cl *LHD/OX* KT22 ....10 C1
St John's Rd *DORK* RH4 ....39 E2
  LHD/OX KT22 ....10 C1
  REDH RH1 ....41 H1
St John's Terrace Rd *REDH* RH1 ....41 H1
St Leonards Rd *EPSOM* KT18 ....6 C4
St Margaret's Rd
  COUL/CHIP CR5 ....16 B1
St Marks Rd *EPSOM* KT18 ....6 C3
St Martins Ms *DORK* RH4 ....40 A1
St Mary's Cl *LHD/OX* KT22 ....9 F3
St Marys Rd *LHD/OX* KT22 ....10 B3
  REIG RH2 ....33 H5
St Matthew's Rd *REDH* RH1 ....34 D3
St Monica's Rd
  KWD/TDW/WH KT20 ....14 B1
St Nicholas Av *GT/LBKH* KT23 ....8 C5
St Nicholas Hl *LHD/OX* KT22 ....10 B2
St Pauls Ms *DORK* RH4 ....40 B2
St Paul's Rd East *DORK* RH4 ....40 B2
St Paul's Rd West *DORK* RH4 ....40 B2
Salbrook Rd *REDH* RH1 ....54 A2
Salfords Ind Est *REDH* RH1 ....54 C3
Sanders Cl *GT/LBKH* KT23 ....8 D3
Sanderstead Cl *LHD/OX* KT22 ....10 A4
Sandcross La *REIG* RH2 ....44 B2
Sandes Pl *LHD/OX* KT22 ....3 E3
Sandhills Rd *REIG* RH2 ....44 C1
Sandlands Gv
  KWD/TDW/WH KT20 ....13 E3
Sandlands Rd
  KWD/TDW/WH KT20 ....13 E3
Sandpit Rd *REDH* RH1 ....34 C5
Sandrock Rd *DORK* RH4 ....38 D3
Sandy La *BRKHM/BTCW* RH3 ....31 G4
  LHD/OX KT22 ....14 C3
  REDH RH1 ....35 H5
  REIG RH2 ....32 C5
Sanders Dr *HORL* RH6 ....56 D4
Sandy Wy *HORL* RH6 ....57 F1
Sangley Rd *HORL* RH6 ....57 G2
Sapte Cl *REDH* RH1 ....34 C5
Sayers Cl *LHD/OX* KT22 ....9 E4
School Hl *REDH* RH1 ....26 C3

School La *DORK* RH4 ....39 F2
  REDH RH1 ....9 F2
  RDKG RH5 ....20 C2
Searle Hl *REIG* RH2 ....44 C1
Second Av
  KWD/TDW/WH KT20 * 24 B1
Seventh Av
  KWD/TDW/WH KT20 * 24 B1
Shabden Cottages
  COUL/CHIP CR5 * 15 H1
Shamrock Cl *LHD/OX* KT22 ....9 F1
Sharon Cl *GT/LBKH* KT23 ....8 C4
Shawley Crs *EPSOM* KT18 ....6 D3
Shawley Wy *EPSOM* KT18 ....6 D3
Sheephouse Gn *RDKG* RH5 ....38 B5
Sheephouse La *RDKG* RH5 ....38 B4
Sheep Wk *REIG* RH2 ....33 F1
Sheldon Cl *REIG* RH2 ....33 H5
Shellwood Dr *RDKG* RH5 ....40 C5
Shellwood Rd *REIG* RH2 ....50 B1
Shelvers Gn
  KWD/TDW/WH KT20 ....13 G1
Shelvers Hl
  KWD/TDW/WH KT20 ....13 F1
Shelvers Sp
  KWD/TDW/WH KT20 ....13 G1
Shelvers Wy
  KWD/TDW/WH KT20 ....13 G1
Shepherd's Hl *REDH* RH1 ....26 C1
Shepherds' Wk *EPSOM* KT18 ....4 B5
Sherborne Cl *EPSOM* KT18 ....6 C2
Shere Cl *RDKG* RH5 ....40 C5
Sheridan Dr *REIG* RH2 ....33 H2
Sheridans Rd *GT/LBKH* KT23 ....19 E1
Sherwood Cl *LHD/OX* KT22 ....9 E3
Sherwood Crs *REIG* RH2 ....44 D3
Shire Pl *REDH* RH1 ....41 H1
Shires Cl *ASHTD* KT21 ....3 H4
Shirley Av *REDH* RH1 ....41 H4
Shortacres *REDH* RH1 ....36 B3
Shrewsbury Rd *REDH* RH1 ....34 C4
Shrubland Rd *BNSTD* SM7 ....7 F1
Sideways La *HORL* RH6 ....56 A5
Silver Cl *KWD/TDW/WH* KT20 ....14 A4
Silverdale Cl *BRKHM/BTCW* RH3 ....41 H3
Silverlea Gdns *HORL* RH6 ....57 G4
Silverstone Cl *REDH* RH1 ....34 D4
Sincots Rd *REDH* RH1 ....34 D4
Sixteenth Av
  KWD/TDW/WH KT20 * 24 B1
Sixth Av *KWD/TDW/WH* KT20 * 24 B1
Skinners La *ASHTD* KT21 ....3 H3
Skipton Wy *HORL* RH6 ....57 F1
Slipshatch Rd *REIG* RH2 ....44 B3
Slipshoe St *REIG* RH2 ....33 F4
Slough La *BRKHM/BTCW* RH3 ....32 A3
  EPSOM 12 A5
Smallfield Rd *HORL* RH6 ....57 F3
Smallmead *HORL* RH6 ....57 F3
Smalls Hill Rd *REIG* RH1 ....51 G5
Smithbarn *HORL* RH6 ....57 F3
The Smithers
  BRKHM/BTCW RH3 ....41 H1
Smith Rd *REIG* RH2 ....44 B2
Smithy Cl *KWD/TDW/WH* KT20 ....24 B1
Smithy La *KWD/TDW/WH* KT20 ....24 B1
Smoke La *REIG* RH2 ....44 D1
Snowerhill Rd
  BRKHM/BTCW RH3 ....42 D3
Solecote *GT/LBKH* KT23 ....8 C5
Sole Farm Av *GT/LBKH* KT23 ....8 B5
Sole Farm Cl *GT/LBKH* KT23 ....8 B4
Sole Farm Rd *GT/LBKH* KT23 ....8 C5
Somerfield Cl
  KWD/TDW/WH KT20 ....7 E4
Somers Cl *REIG* RH2 ....33 G3
Somerset Rd *REDH* RH1 ....41 F1
Somers Rd *REIG* RH2 ....33 G3
Sondes Farm *DORK* RH4 * 39 H1
Sondes Place Cottages
  DORK RH4 * 39 H1
Sondes Place Dr *DORK* RH4 ....39 H1
South Albert Rd *REIG* RH2 ....33 F3
South Close Gn *REDH* RH1 ....26 B4
Southcote Rd *REDH* RH1 ....26 C5
South Downs Wy *RDKG* RH5 ....29 G2
South Dr *RDKG* RH5 ....40 C5
South End *REDH* RH1 ....18 D1
Southern Av *REDH* RH1 ....54 A4
Southern La *COUL/CHIP* CR5 ....15 E4
Southlands Av *HORL* RH6 ....57 E2
South Md *REDH* RH1 ....41 H4
South Pde *HORL* RH6 * 56 D1
  REDH RH1 * 26 C3
South Rd *REIG* RH2 ....33 H5
South Station Ap *REDH* RH1 * 41 H1
South St *DORK* RH4 ....40 A2
South Ter *DORK* RH4 ....40 B2
South View Rd *ASHTD* KT21 ....3 H4

South Wk *REIG* RH2 * 33 H4
Sparrows Md *REDH* RH1 ....35 E1
Spencer Cl *EPSOM* KT18 ....5 E4
Spencer Wy *REDH* RH1 ....46 A4
Spiers Wy *HORL* RH6 ....57 F5
Spindlewoods
  KWD/TDW/WH KT20 ....13 F2
The Spinney *EPSOM* KT18 ....6 B4
  GT/LBKH KT23 ....8 D4
  HORL RH6 ....57 E1
Spital Heath *DORK* RH4 ....29 G5
Spook Hl *RDKG* RH5 ....48 B1
Springcope Rd *REIG* RH2 ....34 A5
Springfield Dr *LHD/OX* KT22 ....2 C4
Springfield Rd *DORK* RH4 ....38 D2
Spring Gv *LHD/OX* KT22 ....8 D3
Springvale Cl *GT/LBKH* KT23 ....18 C1
Spruce Cl *REDH* RH1 ....34 D3
Squirrels Gn *GT/LBKH* KT23 ....8 C3
Stable Cl *EPSOM* KT18 ....5 G4
Stable Ms *REIG* RH2 ....33 G4
Staffords Pl *HORL* RH6 ....57 F4
Stag Leys *ASHTD* KT21 ....4 A5
Staiths Wy *KWD/TDW/WH* KT20 ....6 B5
Staplehurst Cl *REIG* RH2 ....45 E3
Staplehurst Rd *REIG* RH2 ....45 E3
Star La *COUL/CHIP* CR5 ....16 A2
Station Ap *DORK* RH4 ....29 G4
  HORL RH6 ....57 F3
  LHD/OX KT22 ....10 A1
Station Ap East *REDH* RH1 ....45 H1
Station Approach Rd
  KWD/TDW/WH KT20 ....13 G3
Station Ap West *REDH* RH1 ....45 H1
Station Rd *BRKHM/BTCW* RH3 ....31 F3
  DORK RH4 ....40 A1
  HORL RH6 ....57 F3
  LHD/OX KT22 ....10 A1
  REDH RH1 ....26 C3
  REDH RH1 ....34 D3
Station Rd North *REDH* RH1 ....26 C3
Station Rd South *REDH* RH1 ....26 C3
Station Yd
  KWD/TDW/WH KT20 * 14 B1
Stewart *KWD/TDW/WH* KT20 ....13 H1
Stirling Cl *BNSTD* SM7 ....7 F2
Stockfield *HORL* RH6 ....57 F2
Stocks Cl *HORL* RH6 ....57 F4
Stockton Rd *REIG* RH2 ....44 C2
Stoke Cottages *LHD/OX* KT22 * 9 F1
Stoke Ridings
  KWD/TDW/WH KT20 ....13 H3
Stokes Ridings
  KWD/TDW/WH KT20 ....13 H3
Stonecourt Cl *HORL* RH6 ....57 G3
Stonehill Cl *GT/LBKH* KT23 ....8 C5
Stones La *DORK* RH4 ....39 E2
Stoney Cft *COUL/CHIP* CR5 ....16 C2
Stonny Cft *ASHTD* KT21 ....4 B2
Strand Cl *EPSOM* KT18 ....5 F4
Strathcona Av *GT/LBKH* KT23 ....18 A3
Strawson Cft *HORL* RH6 ....56 D2
The Street *ASHTD* KT21 ....4 D2
  BRKHM/BTCW RH3 ....31 F4
  LHD/OX KT22 ....9 F2
Stuart Crs *REIG* RH2 ....44 C2
Stuart Rd *REIG* RH2 ....44 C2
Stubbs La
  KWD/TDW/WH KT20 ....24 B3
Stubs Cl *DORK* RH4 ....40 C3
Stubs Hl *DORK* RH4 ....40 C3
Sturt's La *KWD/TDW/WH* KT20 ....22 D2
Stychens Cl *REDH* RH1 ....37 E3
Stychens La *REDH* RH1 ....37 E3
Styles End *GT/LBKH* KT23 ....18 C2
Subrosa Dr *REDH* RH1 ....26 B5
Subrosa Pk *REDH* RH1 * 26 B5
Suffolk Cl *HORL* RH6 ....57 E4
Summerfield *ASHTD* KT21 ....3 H4
Summerlay Cl
  KWD/TDW/WH KT20 ....14 A1
Summerly Av *REIG* RH2 ....33 G3
Sumner Cl *LHD/OX* KT22 ....9 F4
Sunmead Cl *LHD/OX* KT22 ....9 H2
Sunmead Pde *LHD/OX* KT22 * 10 A2
Sunny Bank *EPSOM* KT18 ....5 E1
Surrey Hills Av
  KWD/TDW/WH KT20 ....31 E1
Sussex Cl *REIG* RH2 ....34 B5
Sutton Gdns *REDH* RH1 ....26 D4
Swallow La *RDKG* RH5 ....48 B2
Swan Mill Gdns *DORK* RH4 ....29 G4
Swanns Meadow
  GT/LBKH KT23 ....18 C1
Swanworth La *RDKG* RH5 ....20 B3
Sycamore Cl *REDH* RH1 * 26 D4
The Sycamores *GT/LBKH* KT23 ....9 E4
Sycamore Wk *REIG* RH2 ....45 E2
Sylvan Wy *REDH* RH1 ....35 F5

T

Tabarin Wy *EW* KT17 ....6 C1
Tadorne Rd
  KWD/TDW/WH KT20 ....13 G1
Tadworth Cl
  KWD/TDW/WH KT20 ....13 H2
Tadworth St
  KWD/TDW/WH KT20 ....13 G3
Talbot Cl *REIG* RH2 ....33 H5
Taleworth Cl *ASHTD* KT21 ....3 H5
Taleworth Pk *ASHTD* KT21 ....3 H5
Taleworth Rd *ASHTD* KT21 ....3 H4
Talfourd Wy *REDH* RH1 ....45 G4
Talisman Wy *EW* KT17 ....6 C1
Tangier Wy
  KWD/TDW/WH KT20 ....7 E2
Tangier Wd
  KWD/TDW/WH KT20 ....7 E3
Tanners Dean *LHD/OX* KT22 ....10 C1
Tanner's Hl *BRKHM/BTCW* RH3 ....41 H1
Tanners Meadow
  BRKHM/BTCW RH3 ....41 H3
The Tannery *REDH* RH1 ....34 C4
Tanyard Wy *HORL* RH6 ....57 F2
Tapner's Rd
  BRKHM/BTCW RH3 ....42 D5
Tarham Cl *HORL* RH6 ....57 F2
Tate Cl *LHD/OX* KT22 ....10 C3
Tattenham Corner Rd
  EPSOM 5 H2
Tattenham Crs *EPSOM* KT18 ....6 B3
Tattenham Gv *EPSOM* KT18 ....6 B4
Tattenham Wy
  KWD/TDW/WH KT20 ....7 E2
Taylor Rd *ASHTD* KT21 ....3 H2
Taynton Dr *REDH* RH1 ....26 D5
Teal Ct *DORK* RH4 * 29 E5
Teazlewood Pk *LHD/OX* KT22 ....3 E2
Temple Wood Dr *REDH* RH1 * 34 D1
Ten Acres Cl *LHD/OX* KT22 ....9 F4
Tenth Av *KWD/TDW/WH* KT20 * 24 B1
Thames Down Link *ASHTD* KT21 ....4 C4
Thatchers Cl *HORL* RH6 ....57 F1
Thepps Cl *REDH* RH1 ....47 F2
Third Av *KWD/TDW/WH* KT20 * 24 B1
Thirteenth Av
  KWD/TDW/WH KT20 * 24 B1
The Thistles *LHD/OX* KT22 ....10 C2
Thistley Cl *COUL/CHIP* CR5 ....16 D2
Thornton Cl *HORL* RH6 ....56 C3
Thornton Pl *HORL* RH6 ....56 C3
The Thoroughfare
  KWD/TDW/WH KT20 ....13 E5
Three Arches Pk *REDH* RH1 * 45 H3
Three Arch Rd *REDH* RH1 ....46 A3
Thurnham Wy
  KWD/TDW/WH KT20 ....6 D5
Tilehurst La *RDKG* RH5 ....41 G2
Tilers Cl *REDH* RH1 ....55 G1
Tiler's Wy *REIG* RH2 ....45 E3
Tilgate Common *REDH* RH1 ....37 G3
Tilley La *EPSOM* KT18 ....12 A3
Timber Cl *GT/LBKH* KT23 ....19 E2
Timber Hl *ASHTD* KT21 ....4 A4
Timperley Gdns *REDH* RH1 ....34 C2
Todds Cl *HORL* RH6 ....56 C5
Tollgate Av *REDH* RH1 ....45 H4
Tollgate Rd *DORK* RH4 ....40 B4
The Topiary *ASHTD* KT21 ....4 A5
Tower Hl *DORK* RH4 ....40 B3
Tower Hill Rd *DORK* RH4 ....40 B3
Tower Rd *KWD/TDW/WH* KT20 ....13 G3
Townfield Rd *DORK* RH4 ....40 A2
Town Md *REDH* RH1 ....37 F3
Townshott Cl *GT/LBKH* KT23 ....18 C3
Tranquil Dl *BRKHM/BTCW* RH3 ....31 H2
Trasher Md *DORK* RH4 ....40 C4
Treadwell Rd *EPSOM* KT18 ....5 G1
Treelands *RDKG* RH5 ....40 C4
Tree View Ct *REIG* RH2 * 34 B4
Treeway *REIG* RH2 ....33 H1
Tregarthen Pl *LHD/OX* KT22 ....10 C1
Trehaven Pde *REIG* RH2 ....44 D2
Trentham Rd *REDH* RH1 ....45 H1
Trindles Rd *REDH* RH1 ....47 F1
Trittons *KWD/TDW/WH* KT20 ....13 G1
Trowers Wy *REDH* RH1 ....35 F1
Trumpetshill Rd
  BRKHM/BTCW RH3 ....32 A5
Tudor Cl *GT/LBKH* KT23 ....8 C4
The Tudors *REIG* RH2 * 33 H4
Tudor Wk *LHD/OX* KT22 ....3 E5
Tugwood Cl *COUL/CHIP* CR5 ....16 D1
Tulyar Cl *KWD/TDW/WH* KT20 ....6 B4
Tumber St *EPSOM* KT18 ....12 A5
Tumblewood Rd *BNSTD* SM7 ....7 E1

Tweed La *BRKHM/BTCW* RH3 ....41 H4
Twelve Acre Cl *GT/LBKH* KT23 ....8 B4
Twelve Av
 KWD/TDW/WH KT20 * 24 B1
Twyner Cl *HORL* RH6 ....57 H2
Tynedale Rd
 BRKHM/BTCW RH3 ....41 H3

U

Underhill Park Rd *REIG* RH2 ....33 G4
Upfield *HORL* RH6 ....57 E5
Upfield Cl *HORL* RH6 ....57 E5
Uplands *ASHTD* KT21 ....3 H5
Upland Wy *EPSOM* KT18 ....6 C4
Upper Bridge Rd *REDH* RH1 ....34 D4
Upper Fairfield Rd
 LHD/OX KT22 ....10 B1
Upper Kiln Dr *RH4* * 40 C3
Upper Lodge Wy
 COUL/CHIP CR5 ....16 D2
Upper Pth *DORK* RH4 * 40 C3
Upper Rose Hl *DORK* RH4 ....40 D2
Upper West St *REIG* RH2 ....33 F4
Usherwood Cl
 KWD/TDW/WH KT20 ....31 E1

V

Vandyke Cl *REDH* RH1 ....34 D2
Vaughan Wy *DORK* RH4 ....40 A1
Vernon Wk *KWD/TDW/WH* KT20 ....6 D5
Vevers Rd *REIG* RH2 ....44 D2
Vicarage Cl *GT/LBKH* KT23 ....8 C5
 KWD/TDW/WH KT20 ....14 A4
Vicarage Gate Ms
 KWD/TDW/WH KT20 * 14 A4
Vicarage La *HORL* RH6 ....56 D2
 LHD/OX KT22 ....10 B2
Vicents Wk *DORK* RH4 ....40 A1
Victoria Cl *HORL* RH6 ....57 E3
Victoria Rd *HORL* RH6 ....57 E3
 REDH RH1 ....35 E5
Victoria Ter *DORK* RH4 * 40 A1
Vincent Cl *LHD/OX* KT22 ....8 D3
Vincent Dr *DORK* RH4 ....40 A2
Vincent La *DORK* RH4 ....40 A1
Vincent Rd *DORK* RH4 ....40 A1
Vincent Wk *DORK* RH4 ....40 A1
Virginia Cl *ASHTD* KT21 ....3 H3
Vogan Cl *REIG* RH2 ....44 D2

W

Walford Rd *RDKG* RH5 ....40 B5
Walkfield Dr *EPSOM* KT18 ....6 B2
Wallace Sq *COUL/CHIP* CR5 ......16 D2
The Walled Gdn
 BRKHM/BTCW RH3 ....31 F5
 KWD/TDW/WH KT20 ....13 H2
Wallis Ms *LHD/OX* KT22 * 10 A2
Walnut Dr *KWD/TDW/WH* KT20 ...14 A4
Walter's Md *ASHTD* KT21 ....4 A2
Walton Rd *EPSOM* KT18 ....12 A1
Walton St *KWD/TDW/WH* KT20 ....13 E4
Wanmer Ct *REIG* RH2 * 33 G3
The Waplings
 KWD/TDW/WH KT20 * 13 F4

Warenne Hts *REDH* RH1 ....45 F1
Warenne Rd *LHD/OX* KT22 ....9 E2
Warltersville Wy *HORL* RH6 ....57 C5
Warren Dr *KWD/TDW/WH* KT20 ...14 C3
Warren Hl *EPSOM* KT18 ....5 F1
Warren Lodge Dr
 KWD/TDW/WH KT20 ....14 A4
Warrenne Rd
 BRKHM/BTCW RH3 ....42 A1
Warrenne Wy *REIG* RH2 ....33 G4
Warren Pk
 KWD/TDW/WH KT20 * 31 E1
Warren Rd *REIG* RH2 ....33 H3
The Warren *ASHTD* KT21 ....4 B5
 KWD/TDW/WH KT20 ....14 A3
Warwick Cl *RDKG* RH5 ....48 B5
Warwick Gdns *ASHTD* KT21 ....3 H2
Warwick Rd *RDKG* RH5 ....48 C5
 REDH RH1 ....34 D3
Warwick Wold Rd *REDH* RH1 ......27 C4
Washington Cl *REIG* RH2 ....33 G2
Wasp Green La *REDH* RH1 ....55 H3
Waterer Gdns
 KWD/TDW/WH KT20 ....7 E3
Waterfield
 KWD/TDW/WH KT20 ....6 B5
Waterfield Gn
 KWD/TDW/WH KT20 ....6 B5
Waterfields *LHD/OX* KT22 ....3 F1
Waterhouse La
 KWD/TDW/WH KT20 ....14 A1
 REDH RH1 ....37 H2
Water La *GT/LBKH* KT23 ....18 A1
Waterlow Rd *REIG* RH2 ....34 A5
Watermead
 KWD/TDW/WH KT20 ....13 F1
Waterside *HORL* RH6 ....57 E1
Waterslade *REDH* RH1 ....34 C4
Waterway Rd *LHD/OX* KT22 ....10 A2
Wathen Rd *DORK* RH4 ....29 F5
Watson Rd *DORK* RH4 ....39 E2
Watts Cl *KWD/TDW/WH* KT20 * ...13 F1
Watt's La *KWD/TDW/WH* KT20 ....13 F1
Watt's Md *KWD/TDW/WH* KT20 ...13 F1
Waverley Pl *LHD/OX* KT22 * 10 B2
The Way *REIG* RH2 ....34 B3
Weald Wy *REIG* RH2 ....45 E3
Weldon Wy *REDH* RH1 ....26 D4
Wellesford Cl *BNSTD* SM7 ....7 F2
Wellhouse Rd
 BRKHM/BTCW RH3 ....42 A2
Wellington Wy *HORL* RH6 ....56 D1
Wells Cl *GT/LBKH* KT23 ....8 A4
Wells Pl *REDH* RH1 ....26 B5
Wenlock Edge *DORK* RH4 * 40 C3
Wesley Cl *HORL* RH6 ....57 E1
 REIG RH2 ....33 F5
Wessels *KWD/TDW/WH* KT20 .....13 H1
West Av *REDH* RH1 ....45 H5
West Bank *DORK* RH4 ....39 H2
Westcott Rd *DORK* RH4 ....39 H1
Westcott St *DORK* RH4 ....38 D2
West Down *GT/LBKH* KT23 ....18 D2
West Dr *KWD/TDW/WH* KT20 ....6 D3
Western Pl *DORK* RH4 * 40 A1
West Farm Av *ASHTD* KT21 ....3 G3
West Farm Cl *ASHTD* KT21 ....3 G4
West Farm Dr *ASHTD* KT21 ....3 H4
Westfield *REIG* RH2 ....33 H1
Westfield Dr *GT/LBKH* KT23 ....8 D2
Westhumble St *RDKG* RH5 ....29 F1
Westleas *HORL* RH6 ....56 C1
Westlees Cl *RDKG* RH5 ....40 D4
Westmead Dr *REDH* RH1 ....54 A2

West Meads *HORL* RH6 ....57 G3
West Rd *REIG* RH2 ....33 H5
West St *DORK* RH4 ....40 A1
 REIG RH2 ....33 F4
Westview Cl *REDH* RH1 ....45 G2
Westway Gdns *REDH* RH1 ....35 E1
Wheatfield Wy *HORL* RH6 ....57 F2
Wheelers La *BRKHM/BTCW* RH3 ...41 H1
Whitebeam Dr *REIG* RH2 ....44 D2
White Beam Wy
 KWD/TDW/WH KT20 ....13 F1
White Bushes *REDH* RH1 ....46 A4
Whitegate Wy
 KWD/TDW/WH KT20 ....6 B5
Whitehall La *REIG* RH2 ....44 B3
White Hl *COUL/CHIP* CR5 ....15 F3
White Lodge Gdns *REDH* RH1 .....54 A2
Whitepost Hl *REDH* RH1 ....34 C4
White Wy *GT/LBKH* KT23 ....18 D1
Whitmore Wy *HORL* RH6 ....56 B2
Wickham Cl *HORL* RH6 ....56 D2
Wiggie La *REDH* RH1 ....35 E2
Wildcroft Dr *RDKG* RH5 ....40 D4
Willey Broom La *CTHM* CR3 ....17 C5
William Evelyn Ct *RDKG* RH5 * 38 B4
Willowbank Gdns
 KWD/TDW/WH KT20 ....13 F2
Willow Brean *HORL* RH6 ....56 C2
Willow Ct *HORL* RH6 * 54 B5
Willow Md *DORK* RH4 ....29 E5
Willow Rd *REDH* RH1 ....45 G2
Willow V *LHD/OX* KT22 ....8 D3
Willow Wk *KWD/TDW/WH* KT20 ...21 H5
 REDH RH1 ....46 B1
Wilmerhatch La *EPSOM* KT18 ....4 D2
Wilmots Cl *REIG* RH2 ....34 A3
Wilsons *KWD/TDW/WH* KT20 ......13 H1
Wilton Rd *REDH* RH1 ....34 D5
Wimborne Av *REDH* RH1 ....45 H4
Windermere Wy *REIG* RH2 ....34 A4
Windmill Cl *HORL* RH6 ....57 F3
Windmill Dr *LHD/OX* KT22 ....10 B3
 REIG RH2 ....34 B2
Windmill Wy *REIG* RH2 ....34 B2
Wither Dl *HORL* RH6 ....56 C2
Withey Brook *HORL* RH6 ....56 B5
Withey Mdw *HORL* RH6 ....56 B5
The Withies *LHD/OX* KT22 ....3 F5
Withybed Cnr
 KWD/TDW/WH KT20 ....13 F3
Wolvens La *RDKG* RH5 ....38 C5
Wolverton Cl *HORL* RH6 ....56 D5
Wolverton Gdns *HORL* RH6 ....56 D4
Wonford Cl
 KWD/TDW/WH KT20 ....23 E1
Wonham La *BRKHM/BTCW* RH3 ...31 H5
Woodbridge Av *LHD/OX* KT22 ....3 E5
Woodbridge Gv *LHD/OX* KT22 ......3 E5
Wood Cl *REDH* RH1 ....54 A3
Woodcote Hrst *HORL* RH6 ....57 F2
Woodcote Green Rd
 EPSOM KT18 ....5 E1
Woodcote Hurst *EPSOM* KT18 .....5 E1
Woodcote Park Rd *EPSOM* KT18 ...5 E1
Woodcote Side *EPSOM* KT18 ....5 E1
Woodcrest Wk *REIG* RH2 ....34 C2
Woodend *LHD/OX* KT22 ....10 C5
Woodfield *ASHTD* KT21 ....3 H2
Woodfield Cl *ASHTD* KT21 ....3 H2
 REDH RH1 ....34 C3
Woodfield La *ASHTD* KT21 ....4 A2
Woodfield Rd *ASHTD* KT21 ....3 H2
Woodfield Wy *REDH* RH1 ....34 C3
Woodgavil *BNSTD* SM7 ....7 F1

Woodhatch Rd *REIG* RH2 ....45 F3
Woodhayes *HORL* RH6 ....57 F2
Woodlands *ASHTD* KT21 * 4 B5
 HORL RH6 ....57 G2
Woodlands Av *REDH* RH1 ....34 D5
Woodlands Copse *ASHTD* KT21 .....3 H1
Woodlands Ct *REDH* RH1 * 4 A5
Woodlands Gdns *EPSOM* KT18 .....6 C2
Woodlands Pk
 KWD/TDW/WH KT20 ....30 D1
Woodlands Rd *GT/LBKH* KT23 .....18 B5
 LHD/OX KT22 ....2 B3
 REDH RH1 ....45 H1
Woodlands Wy *ASHTD* KT21 ....4 C1
 KWD/TDW/WH KT20 ....22 A1
Woodland Wy
 KWD/TDW/WH KT20 ....14 B2
Wood La *KWD/TDW/WH* KT20 .....7 F2
Woodroyd Av *HORL* RH6 ....56 D3
Woodroyd Gdns *HORL* RH6 ....56 D3
Woodside *KWD/TDW/WH* KT20 ...24 B1
 LHD/OX KT22 ....8 D5
Woodside Wy *REDH* RH1 ....46 A4
Wood St *REDH* RH1 ....26 C5
Woodview Cl *ASHTD* KT21 ....4 C1
Woodville Rd *LHD/OX* KT22 ....3 F5
Woolborough La *REDH* RH1 ....55 F5
Wootton Cl *EPSOM* KT18 ....5 E1
Worcester Rd *REIG* RH2 ....33 C4
Wordsworth Md *REDH* RH1 ....5 E1
Worlds End *EPSOM* KT18 * 5 F1
Worple Rd *LHD/OX* KT22 ....10 B3
Worsted Gn *REDH* RH1 ....26 D5
Wotton Dr *RDKG* RH5 ....38 A4
Wray Common Rd *REIG* RH2 ....34 B2
Wrayfield Av *REIG* RH2 ....34 A1
Wraylands Dr *REIG* RH2 ....34 B1
Wray La *REIG* RH2 ....34 B1
Wraymead Pl *REIG* RH2 * 33 H1
Wray Mill Pk *REIG* RH2 ....34 B1
Wray Park Rd *REIG* RH2 ....33 H1
Wyecliffe Gdns *REDH* RH1 ....26 C5
Wysemead *HORL* RH6 ....57 G3

Y

Yardley Cl *REIG* RH2 ....33 G3
Yarm Cl *LHD/OX* KT22 ....10 A1
Yarm Court Rd *LHD/OX* KT22 .....10 A1
Yarm Wy *LHD/OX* KT22 ....10 A1
Yattendon Rd *HORL* RH6 ....57 E3
Yeats Cl *REDH* RH1 ....45 H2
Yeomans Cft *GT/LBKH* KT23 ....8 C5
Yeoman Wy *REDH* RH1 ....46 A4
Yew Tree Bottom Rd *EW* KT17 ......6 A1
Yew Tree Cl *HORL* RH6 ....57 E3
Yew Tree La *REIG* RH2 ....33 H2
Yew Tree Rd *DORK* RH4 ....29 G3
Yorke Gdns *REIG* RH2 ....33 G3
Yorke Rd *REIG* RH2 ....33 G3
Young St *LHD/OX* KT22 ....9 E5

Z

Zig Zag Rd *KWD/TDW/WH* KT20 ...29 H2
 RDKG RH5 ....20 B3

Index - featured places

Aberdour School
 KWD/TDW/WH KT20 ....7 F3
Acorns CE School
 REIG RH2 ....43 E5
The Acorns First School
 BRKHM/BTCW RH3 ....31 F4
All Saints CE Infant School
 LHD/OX KT22 ....3 E4
Archway Theatre
 HORL RH6 ....57 E4
The Ashcombe School
 DORK RH4 ....29 F4
Ashtead Clinic
 ASHTD KT21 ....4 A2
Ashtead CC
 ASHTD KT21 ....4 A2
Ashtead Hospital
 ASHTD KT21 ....4 A5

Astra Business Centre
 REDH RH1 ....54 A4
Banstead Athletic FC
 KWD/TDW/WH KT20 ....6 C5
Banstead County Junior
 School
 BNSTD SM7 ....7 F1
Banstead Sports Centre
 KWD/TDW/WH KT20 ....6 C5
Barnett Wood Infant School
 ASHTD KT21 ....3 H2
Beacon School
 BNSTD SM7 ....7 E2
Belfry Shopping Centre
 REDH RH1 ....34 D3
Best Western Gatwick Moat
 House Hotel
 HORL RH6 ....56 C5

Best Western Reigate Manor
 Hotel *REIG* RH2 ....33 G1
Betchworth Park Golf Club
 DORK RH4 ....30 A5
Bletchingley Golf Club
 REDH RH1 ....37 F3
Bocketts Farm Park
 LHD/OX KT22 ....9 H5
Bookham Grange Hotel
 GT/LBKH KT23 ....8 A3
Bookham Industrial Estate
 GT/LBKH KT23 ....8 B3
Box Hill Country Park
 KWD/TDW/WH KT20 ....30 A2
Box Hill School
 RDKG RH5 ....20 B2
Brambletye Junior School
 REDH RH1 ....46 A1

Bramley School
 KWD/TDW/WH KT20 ....13 ..
Bridge Industrial Estate
 HORL RH6 ....5?
Brockham School
 BRKHM/BTCW RH3 ....4..
Brooklands School
 REIG RH2 ....4..
Burghwood Clinic
 BNSTD SM7 ....7..
Burstow Lodge Business Centre
 HORL RH6 ....5..
Burys Court School
 REIG RH2 ....4..
Business Park 5
 LHD/OX KT22 ....
Chinthurst School
 KWD/TDW/WH KT20 ....

Chipstead RFC
   COUL/CHIP CR5 ....15 H1
City of London Freemens
   School
   ASHTD KT21 ....4 D4
Community & Adult Education
   Centre
   HORL RH6 ....56 C3
Corner House Hotel
   HORL RH6 ....56 D4
Cornfield School
   REDH RH1 ....45 H4
Crouch Industrial Estate
   LHD/OX KT22 ....3 E4
Dawnay CP School
   GT/LBKH KT23 ....8 C5
Denbies Wine Estate
   RDKG RH5 ....29 F2
Donyngs Recreation Centre
   REDH RH1 ....34 C3
Doods Brow School
   REDH RH1 ....36 B3
The Dorking Business Park
   DORK RH4 ....29 E5
Dorking Cemetery
   DORK RH4 ....29 G4
Dorking FC (Meadowbank)
   DORK RH4 ....29 E5
Dorking General Hospital
   DORK RH4 ....40 A2
Dorking Golf Club
   RDKG RH5 ....40 C2
Dorking Halls
   DORK RH4 ....29 G5
Dorking Lawn Tennis &
   Squash Club
   DORK RH4 ....40 A3
Dorking Museum
   DORK RH4 ....40 A1
Dorking RFC
   BRKHM/BTCW RH3 ....30 D4
Dorking Swimming & Sports
   Centre
   DORK RH4 ....29 G5
Downs View School
   REIG RH2 ....45 E3
Downsend School -
   Ashtead Lodge
   SHTD KT21 ....4 A3
Downsend School-
   Leatherhead Lodge
   LHD/OX KT22 ....3 G5
Dottar School
   REIG RH2 ....34 B5
Elmswood Infant School
   REDH RH1 ....35 E5
East Surrey College
   REDH RH1 ....26 A5
   REDH RH1 ....35 E1
East Surrey Hospital
   REDH RH1 ....46 B3
Fenwick Infant School
   GT/LBKH KT23 ....8 D4
Fenwick Junior School
   GT/LBKH KT23 ....8 D4
Effingham Community Sports
   Centre
   EHSLY KT24 ....18 A2
Epsom Cemetery
   EPSOM KT18 ....5 G1
Epsom Downs Racecourse
   EPSOM KT18 ....5 H2
Fairfield Medical Centre
   GT/LBKH KT23 ....18 D1
Fetcham Social & Sports
   Club
   LHD/OX KT22 ....9 G1
Fetcham Village Infant
   School
   LHD/OX KT22 ....9 F2
Fitzgarry Farm Business
   Park
   REIG RH2 ....53 E3
Furzefield Primary School
   REDH RH1 ....26 D3
Garston Park Business
   Centre
   REDH RH1 ....26 B5
Gatwick Park Hospital
   HORL RH6 ....56 C4
Gatwick Driving Range
   HORL RH6 ....46 A4
Great Bookham County Infant
   School
   GT/LBKH KT23 ....18 C1
Grove House School
   ASHTD KT21 ....4 B2
Hanbury Industrial Estate
   RDKG RH4 ....29 E5

The Hawthorns School
   REDH RH1 ....36 D1
Heath Business Centre
   REDH RH1 ....54 B4
Heathcote Medical Centre
   KWD/TDW/WH KT20 ....13 H2
Hockley Industrial Centre
   REDH RH1 ....34 D5
Holmesdale School
   REIG RH2 ....33 H2
Holmethorpe Industrial
   Estate
   REDH RH1 ....35 F1
Horley Anderson Centre
   HORL RH6 ....56 C3
Horley Health Centre
   HORL RH6 ....57 E3
Horley Infant School
   HORL RH6 ....57 E3
Hyland Business Centre
   REDH RH1 ....34 D4
Kingsfield Business Centre
   REDH RH1 ....35 E5
Kingswood Golf Club
   KWD/TDW/WH KT20 ....14 C4
Kingswood Primary School
   KWD/TDW/WH KT20 ....24 B3
Langshott County Infant
   School
   HORL RH6 ....57 G3
Langshott Manor Hotel
   HORL RH6 ....57 H1
Leatherhead & Dorking
   Gymnastics Club
   LHD/OX KT22 ....10 A3
Leatherhead Business Park
   LHD/OX KT22 ....3 F4
Leatherhead Clinic
   LHD/OX KT22 ....10 C1
Leatherhead CC
   LHD/OX KT22 ....10 A2
Leatherhead FC
   LHD/OX KT22 ....10 A2
Leatherhead Golf Club
   LHD/OX KT22 ....3 E1
Leatherhead Hospital
   LHD/OX KT22 ....10 C2
Leatherhead Industrial
   Estate
   LHD/OX KT22 ....10 A1
Leatherhead Institute
   LHD/OX KT22 ....10 B1
Leatherhead Leisure Centre &
   Water Park
   LHD/OX KT22 ....10 A3
Leatherhead Museum
   LHD/OX KT22 ....10 B2
Macdonald Burford Bridge
   Hotel
   RDKG RH5 ....29 G1
Macdonald White Horse
   Hotel
   DORK RH4 ....40 B4
Manorfield Primary
   School
   HORL RH6 ....56 D3
Manor House School
   GT/LBKH KT23 ....18 A2
Meath Green Infant
   School
   HORL RH6 ....56 D1
Meath Green Junior
   School
   HORL RH6 ....56 D1
Merland Rise Primary
   School
   EPSOM KT18 ....6 C4
Merstham Primary School
   REDH RH1 ....26 C3
Mole Business Park
   LHD/OX KT22 ....10 A1
Ashtead Common National
   Nature Reserve
   ASHTD KT21 ....3 H1
New Lodge School
   DORK RH4 ....29 F3
North Holmwood CC
   RDKG RH5 ....48 C1
Nutfield Cemetery
   REDH RH1 ....35 H3
Nutfield Church CE Primary
   School
   REDH RH1 ....36 B5
Nutfield Priory Hotel
   REDH RH1 ....35 G4
Nutley Dean Business Centre
   HORL RH6 ....52 A5
Oakfield Junior School
   LHD/OX KT22 ....9 F3

Oakwood School
   HORL RH6 ....57 F3
Oakwood Sports Centre
   HORL RH6 ....57 G3
Orchard Business Centre
   REDH RH1 ....54 A3
Orchards Community Infant
   School
   REIG RH2 ....44 C2
Pachesham Park Golf Centre
   LHD/OX KT22 ....2 C3
Parsons Mead School
   ASHTD KT21 ....4 A4
Perrywood Business Park
   REDH RH1 ....54 B2
Pitwood Park Industrial Estate
   KWD/TDW/WH KT20 ....6 D5
Pixham School
   DORK RH4 ....29 G4
Plough Industrial Estate
   LHD/OX KT22 ....3 E5
Polesden Lacey (NT)
   RDKG RH5 ....18 C5
Powell Corderoy Primary
   School
   DORK RH4 ....39 H2
Premier Cinema
   DORK RH4 ....29 G5
Premier Travel Inn
   HORL RH6 ....56 D5
   KWD/TDW/WH KT20 ....7 E4
   REDH RH1 ....54 A1
The Priory CE Voluntary
   Aided School
   DORK RH4 ....59 H2
Quarryside Business Park
   REDH RH1 ....26 B5
Queen Elizabeth's Foundation
   Training College
   LHD/OX KT22 ....2 B2
Rainbow Natural Health
   Centre
   REDH RH1 ....34 D5
Randalls Park Crematorium
   LHD/OX KT22 ....2 C5
Redhill Aerodrome
   REDH RH1 ....47 E4
Redhill Business Centre
   REDH RH1 ....34 D3
Redhill College
   REDH RH1 ....35 F5
Redhill FC
   REDH RH1 ....45 H3
Redhill & Reigate Golf Club
   REDH RH1 ....45 F2
The Redlands Primary
   School
   DORK RH4 ....40 B4
Redstone Cemetery
   REDH RH1 ....35 F5
Reigate College
   REIG RH2 ....33 H3
Reigate Day Hospital
   REDH RH1 ....34 B4
Reigate Grammar School
   REIG RH2 ....34 A4
Reigate Heath Golf Club
   REIG RH2 ....32 C4
Reigate Hill Golf Club
   REIG RH2 ....26 A3
Reigate Parish Infant School
   REIG RH2 ....34 A4
Reigate Priory Junior School
   REIG RH2 ....33 G4
Reigate Priory & Museum
   REIG RH2 ....33 G4
Reigate St Mary's Preparatory
   & Choir School
   REIG RH2 ....33 H4
Reigate School
   REIG RH2 ....45 E2
The Royal Alexandra & Albert
   School
   REIG RH2 ....25 G4
Rydon Business Centre
   LHD/OX KT22 ....3 E5
Ryebrook Business Park
   LHD/OX KT22 ....3 E5
St Andrews Catholic School
   LHD/OX KT22 ....3 G5
St Annes Catholic Primary
   School
   BNSTD SM7 ....7 G1
St Bedes School
   REDH RH1 ....34 C1
St Catherine's Primary
   School
   REDH RH1 ....37 F3
St Giles CE (Aided) Infant

   School
   ASHTD KT21 ....4 B3
St Johns Primary School
   REDH RH1 ....45 G1
St Johns School
   LHD/OX KT22 ....10 B1
St Josephs Catholic Primary
   School
   REDH RH1 ....34 C3
St Josephs RC Primary School
   DORK RH4 ....40 A1
St Margaret's School
   KWD/TDW/WH KT20 ....13 H1
St Martins CE Primary School
   DORK RH4 ....28 D5
St Martins Walk Shopping
   Centre
   DORK RH4 ....29 F5
St Marys CE Infant School
   LHD/OX KT22 ....10 C2
St Matthews CE Primary
   School
   REDH RH1 ....34 D2
St Michaels CE First School
   RDKG RH5 ....20 C2
St Nicholas School
   REDH RH1 ....26 D4
St Pauls CE Aided Primary
   School
   REDH RH1 ....40 B1
St Peter & Paul CE Infant School
   CTHM CR3 ....17 G5
St Peters RC Primary School
   LHD/OX KT22 ....3 G5
Salfords Industrial Estate
   REDH RH1 ....54 A2
Salfords Primary School
   REDH RH1 ....46 A5
Sandcross Junior School
   REIG RH2 ....44 B2
The Screen at Reigate
   REIG RH2 ....33 G4
Shawley Primary School
   EPSOM KT18 ....6 C3
South Bookham School
   GT/LBKH KT23 ....19 E2
Southern Clinic
   REIG RH2 ....34 A5
South Nutfield CC
   REDH RH1 ....47 F1
Starhurst School
   RDKG RH5 ....40 C3
Sturt Priory Hospital
   KWD/TDW/WH KT20 ....23 E1
Surrey Downs Golf Club
   KWD/TDW/WH KT20 ....15 E2
Surrey National Golf Club
   CTHM CR3 ....17 H3
The Swan Centre
   LHD/OX KT22 ....10 B1
Tadworth Primary School
   KWD/TDW/WH KT20 ....13 H2
Tattenham Health Centre
   EPSOM KT18 ....6 B3
Theatre Magenta
   LHD/OX KT22 ....3 E4
Therfield School
   LHD/OX KT22 ....3 E4
Thistle Hotel
   HORL RH6 ....57 E1
Thorncroft Manor
   LHD/OX KT22 ....10 A3
Travelodge
   DORK RH4 ....29 G5
   LHD/OX KT22 ....10 A2
Tudors Business Centre
   KWD/TDW/WH KT20 ....14 B2
Tyrrells Wood Golf Club
   LHD/OX KT22 ....11 F4
Vale Primary School
   EPSOM KT18 ....5 F4
Walton Heath Golf Club
   Shop
   KWD/TDW/WH KT20 ....13 F5
Walton on the Hill CE Junior
   School
   KWD/TDW/WH KT20 ....13 E5
Walton on the Hill Primary
   School
   KWD/TDW/WH KT20 ....13 F4
Warwick Quadrant & Harlequin
   Theatre, Cinema & Library
   REDH RH1 ....35 E3
The Warwick School
   REDH RH1 ....35 F3
West Ashtead Primary School
   ASHTD KT21 ....3 H5
Westcott CE First School
   DORK RH4 ....39 E2

Acknowledgements

Schools address data provided by Education Direct.

Petrol station information supplied by Johnsons

One-way street data provided by © Tele Atlas N.V. Tele Atlas

Garden centre information provided by

Garden Centre Association Britains best garden centres

Wyevale Garden Centres

The statement on the front cover of this atlas is sourced, selected and quoted from a reader comment and feedback form received in 2004

How do I find the perfect place?

AA Lifestyle Guides
Britain's largest travel publisher
order online at www.theAA.com/travel